美高新鲜事
Behind The Scenes

陈贝婷
Beiting (Betty) Chen / 著

文汇出版社

目 录
Content

前　言
Foreword

Megan Wang

（哈佛法学院法律博士，南加州大学
前大中华地区招生负责人）

当招生官那些年，常被问到"去美国念书好不好"。此问题的困难度不亚于另一个不常见，但同样经典的"美国天气咋样"。既然没有一个答案能覆盖美国 50 个州一年 365 天的寒暑交替，当然也没有一个答案能适用于国内数以万计，从小学到博士后的普罗求学大众。看到这里，有些读者立即聪明地缩小了问题范围，改成"我/我家孩子该不该去美国念初中/高中/大学/研究院"。每次遇见这问题，我只能面带微笑，给出一个看似说了等于没说的官方答案：那得看你/你家孩子。

大众现今有许多机会和渠道了解美国的教育及文化，此类书籍、文章、报道、热帖数不胜数。这些信息来源大多有既定的观点和定论，对异国求学一事非褒即贬，通篇的道理和说辞。对于留学生活本身，它们却极少提供中立而细致的描述，可以让读者自己感受并评估真实的留学生涯。

正因如此，贝婷的这本书才弥足珍贵。书中巨细靡遗地描述种种留学中的校园内外事物，其角度不是一个回想当年的成年人，而是一个尚在求学的青葱少女，字里行间满是豆蔻年华独有的好奇心和求知欲。小姑娘会为功课烦恼，为活动奔走，为舞会兴奋，为朋友加油。常言道：以小见大，书中所述看似琐碎小事，却最实际地反映出中美教育和文化的差异和相似。

身为移居海外的过来人和教育者，我一直认为留学生涯里最重要和艰难的不是刻苦学习或成绩优秀，而是如何培养在异国他乡生活的能力。相对于知识传达，美国教育更注重能力培养。书中常提到的课堂上小组合作，学生自我评分，甚至最基本的美式走班制都意欲培养学生的各种能力，例如人际交往、合作诚信、时间管理，当然还有西方教育的核心——独立思考和批判思维。

留学他乡的过程本就五味陈杂，种种滋味，难与外人道。贝婷把她自己这几年的体验撰写成一杯纯净的水，不掺鸡汤，不撒狗血，更没加油添醋。正因其纯粹，读者方能自己去感受东西方的文化差异，并思考美国教育是否适合自己或家人。书中所写之事看似平淡无奇的一滴水，但波澜壮阔的人生海洋不正是由无数颗水滴积累而成的吗？

对于有意留学的学生和家长，贝婷的这本书虽未能解答"美国天气如何"这道难题，但希望对于大家心里的另一个问题有所启发及帮助。

During my years as an admissions officer, I often faced the infamous question: "Is studying in America a good idea?" This is a question as challenging as another less frequently asked but no less serious one, namely "How's the weather in America?" As there is no single forecast that could encompass all 50 states and 365 days of changing weather patterns, there is no one recommendation that is applicable to the tens of thousands of potential Chinese students ranging from elementary school children to post-doctoral candidates. Some readers may wisely narrow the question to "is going to American for elementary school/junior high/high school/college/graduate school a good idea for me/my child." Every time I heard this variation of the question, I simply smiled and offered the enigmatic answer: that depends on you/your child.

In this time and age of information proliferation, the Chinese public has many opportunities to learn about the American education system and cultural environment. Though there are countless publications, articles, stories and social media posts on this subject matter, most of them have presupposed perspectives, where they either support or object to the idea of studying abroad. While they elaborate endlessly on their own opinions, these sources offer few objective, realistic and detailed descriptions of a student's life in America.

This is precisely why this little memoir from Betty is so invaluable. Inside these pages are thorough narration of an ordinary girl's daily life revolving around her school, teachers and friends. The perspective is that of a teenager student recording her present life, not an adult reminiscing about days past. These stories reflect the singularly inquisitive nature of an adolescent. Her daily excitements and worries, challenges and discoveries, are at once singular to her and yet universal to all 17-year-olds. These seemingly insignificant moments and lessons provide the readers a telling and genuine reflections of the underlying differences and similarities between the East and the West.

As a Chinese American who was once a receiver and later a participant in the American education system, I firmly believe that the greatest challenge for a foreign student is neither completing the schoolwork nor achieving stellar grades, but rather successfully adapting to a new social and cultural environment. American education emphasizes the development of abilities more than the mastery of knowledge. In her book, Betty often mentions group projects, self evaluations, even the ubiquitous American practice of classroom assignment; these are all designed to cultivate various personal skills in the students, be it social interaction, honesty and collaboration, time management, and the core of Western education – independent thinking and critical analysis.

Studying abroad is in and of itself an emotional and audacious journey that can seldom be described clearly to outsiders. Betty has tried to distill her experiences into a glass of clear water, with no additives, judgments or presumptions, to give the readers clear and objective insights into the life of a student abroad. I hope Betty's story can inspire the readers to evaluate and appreciate the differences and similarities between the two cultures, and decide for themselves whether to pursue their futures in America.

For those students and parents interested in America, this book unfortunately does not answer the question of "How's the weather in the U. S?" but hopefully it will provide some insights and inspirations to the other key question on your minds.

Megan Wang

Harvard Law School, Juris Doctor

University of Southern California, former admission director for Greater China region

与好友聚餐（左一是Charlie，左二是Megan，左三是妈妈，右一是爸爸，右二是我。）Megan是本书前言的作者，南加州大学前大中华区招生负责人。

Lunch with friends and family (Left one is Charlie; Left two is Megan; Left three is my mother; Right one is my father; Right two is me.) Megan also wrote the foreword for *Behind The Scenes* who was the former admission director for Greater China region for University of Southern California.

豪叔为我写的书法。他是我学习路上的引导人，为我指点迷津。

Calligraphy written by Howard Cheng who sheds the light and leads the way on my learning journey.

我 11 年级学术荣誉生颁奖典礼（从左到右分别为：顾问、我、校长）。此奖项颁发给 9—11 年级平均成绩点数计算（GPA）超过 4.0 的学生。

Junior Awards Night (From the left: counselor, I, School Principal). The Academic Letter with Honor is given to Juniors with cumulative GPA higher than 4.0.

我有幸在 11 年级的暑假参加在纽约大学举办的 GSTEM 暑期项目，鼓励 11 年级的女孩子探索 STEM 的相关领域，这其中包括与科学、科技、工程及数学导师共同做项目。我还获得了 GSTEM 的数据分析奖学金，将与亚马逊的数据工程师一起用大数据预测房价走向。

I have the chance to participate in the NYU GSTEM program which provides opportunities for uprising senior girls to work along with a STEM field mentor to complete a STEM(Science, Technology, Engineering, Math) related project. I also receive the Winston Data Scholarship to cover the program cost and works with Amazon's applied scientist, Rob Barton, to predict home prices and compete for $1 million prize by improving Zillow's Zestimate algorithm.

我在纽约大学（美国唯一一座位于纽约心脏地带的私立名校）的标志前留影。纽约大学的教学楼及宿舍遍布曼哈顿下城的华盛顿广场及格林尼治村。纽约大学有世界闻名的 Stern 商学院及美国排名第一的应用数学研究机构——Courant 数学科学研究所，也是我此次暑期项目的举办地。

I am standing in front of the classic New York University (the only private institute in the heart of New York City) logo. NYU's buildings spread out across Washington Square Park and Greenwich Village area. NYU is known for its Stern School of Business and Courant Institute of Mathematical Sciences, the #1 school in applied math, where my data science summer program takes place.

我通过暑假访问位于纽约曼哈顿上城的哥伦比亚大学，并在其标志性的图书馆前留影。哥伦比亚大学的著名校友包括 5 位美国开国元勋，以及奥巴马、罗斯福等 4 位美国总统。

I have the opportunity to visit the Columbia University in upper Manhattan and take a picture in front of its iconic library. Columbia's alumni include 5 founding fathers of the U.S. and 4 Presidents of the U.S. including Barack Obama and Franklin Roosevelt.

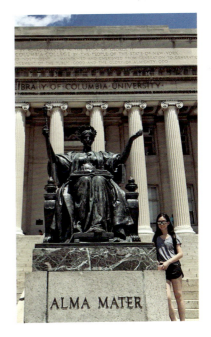

11 年级的春假期间，我前往北加州探访斯坦福。利用假期访问大学是美国高中学生的必修课，大学环境直接影响 12 年级申请时的选择与目标。

I visited Stanford University during Junior year's spring break. College visit is an important activity for all American high school students because it directly effects their choices and goals when they apply for colleges.

我与斯坦福的学霸们在斯坦福大学的冥想室合影。斯坦福大学为了给学生营造一个安静不受打扰的思考环境，建造了一个充满阳光与植物的开放空间。

Picture with Stanford students in the iconic Windhover. This room was built for students to meditate and isolate from the crowded environment filled with sun light and plants so that they can think out loud without distractions.

我在北加州访问斯坦福大学的同时，还有幸访问了加州大学伯克利分校。与学霸们聊学习，聊就业，探讨如何在美国立足成为世界公民。
I got to meet smart Berkeley students while visiting colleges in Northern California in a Chinese restaurant. (aka. Berkeley students' second cafeteria) Blessed with the opportunity to discuss Berkeley's college life, employment, and how Chinese keep a foothold in the U.S. and become global citizens.

住在 Newport Beach 的我可以周末访校一日游，在南加州大学做个游客。
Tourist @ USC on weekend. I have the privilege to visit USC in a one-hour drive as a resident of Newport Beach.

我在南加州大学 Annenberg 传媒学院留影。USC Annenberg 传播与新闻学院作为全美传媒专业类排名第一的院校备受瞩目。

Typical tourist picture in front of Annenberg School for Communication and Journalism @ USC. Annenberg School for Communication and Journalism gains its fame as the #1 school for communication in the nation.

南加州的夕阳，也是我住在海滨城市的特别福利。

Surreal sunset @ Balboa Island. Watching sunset by the ocean is my privilege as a girl who lives in Newport Beach.

我周末的日常活动：玩水。
Go to the beach on weekends is one of my regular activities as a Newport girl who lives close to the water.

我是一位不折不扣的爱狗人士，不仅自己养了只小狗，还不忘与朋友家的狗玩耍。（从左到右：乌冬、我与布鲁斯、Coco）
I am also the biggest dog lover who does not only have a dog but also love to play with friend's dogs. (From left to right: Udon, Bruce & I, Coco)

校园一角，近两年全新建造的大剧院。
A corner of the CdM campus with the new theater built recently.

学校的游泳池充当了物理课纸船比赛场地。
Swimming pool functions as the location for swimming and water polo practices and the playing field for Physics classes' boat races every year.

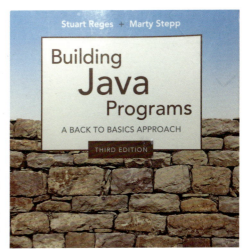

计算机科学的教科书，一本超过 1000 页的基础 Java 教程。

Textbook for AP Computer Science, a foundational Java textbook with over 1000 pages.

同学们在课堂上讨论题目，协作解决编程时遇到的困难。

Students are discussing computer science project in class. AP Computer Science class requires a high level of discussion and cooperation between students to solve difficult problems while coding.

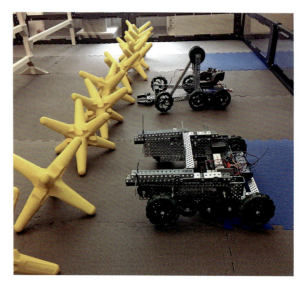

我和 AP Computer Science 的同学在 AP 考试后一起造机器人，为参加学区比赛做准备，同时也作为考后的放松。

I built Vex Robots with AP Computer Science classmates after AP exam as a preparation for school district's robot competition and relaxation after a big test.

AP 英语的阅读作业，通过阅读理解及课堂讨论为 AP 考试做准备。

Reading assignments in AP Language and Composition class prepare for the AP exam through readings and discussions.

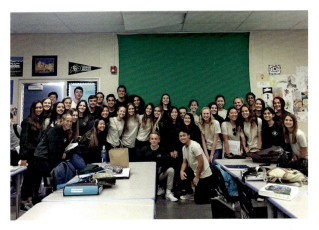

我与 AYS 的小伙伴们。AYS 作为学校的五大领袖组织之一，成为学生与社区服务的桥梁。

My At Your Service family bridges between the students and community by offering meaningful community service opportunities as one of the five leadership clubs on campus.

我在印第安纳大学 HSJI 传媒夏令营课上结交的新朋友。

I made new friends in the Multimedia class at High School Journalism Institute took place in Indiana University's Media School.

Diamond Bar High School 开学前夕领书盛况，书本排列整齐，使大量学生返校领书时的秩序井井有条。

Picking up books before school starts in Diamond Bar High School. All the textbooks are perfectly lined up in order to speed up the book distributing process with thousands of students.

Scores per Category

Category:	Weight:	
Homework	15%	
Participation	5%	数学成绩占比
Quiz	10%	Precalculus weighting
Test	70%	

Scores per Category

Category:	Weight:	
Assignment	10%	
Labs	25%	化学成绩占比
Quizzes	10%	Chemistry weighting
Unit Tests	45%	

Scores per Category

Category:	Weight:	
Classwork/Homework	25%	
Integrity	5%	英语成绩占比
Quiz/Test	10%	English weighting
Socratic Seminar and Projects	20%	
Writing	40%	

11 年级部分课程占比举例，每门课程都有着不同的侧重点。

Score weighting examples from Junior year's courses. The amount of weight determines the importance of a specific category in the class.

以 1920 年代《了不起的盖茨比》为主题的冬季舞会在学校举办的预热活动。
Winter Formal event at the school based on the Roaring 20's theme inspired by *The Great Gatsby.*

因"签证风波"离我而去的加勒比邮轮。
The Caribbean cruise that left me behind after the student VISA tragedy.

人头攒动的 DBHS 开放日，各大学科部门都使出浑身解数吸引家长及学生的目光。
Crowded Open House night @ DBHS. All departments use special strategies to attract parents and students.

历史课上异想天开的团队手工作业——运河。我与同学利用课余时间共同完成历史课上的项目。
The group project in World History class: Canal. My teammates and I devote our time after school to complete the project.

学生利用课余时间为社团画海报，宣传社团举办的特殊活动。
Students are promoting their club by making big posters after school for their upcoming special events.

我十年级英语课最爱的课外读物：*China Rich Girlfriend*（《中国富豪女友》）以及 *The Knockoff*（《仿造品》）。
My favorite novels from 10th grade English class's individual reading assignments: *Chinese Rich Girlfriend* and *The knockoff*.

CdM 校园的雨后清晨有不同寻常的蔚蓝天空。
CdM's extraordinary morning view after a rainy night with bright blue sky.

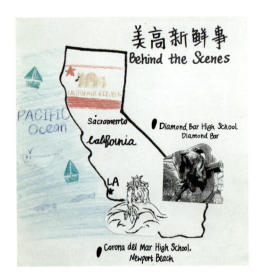

本书封套设计灵感来自于我，由设计师赵军叔叔完成精美的后期制作。
Cover design was completed with my personal ideas and Uncle Zhao's amazing production.

两个学校背后的那些故事

身边有许许多多的人来问我到底是 DBHS（Diamond Bar High School）好还是新学校 CdM（Corona del Mar High School）好，我只能说，两家都好（这个问题就好比长辈问小朋友更喜欢爸爸还是妈妈）。DBHS 是一个亚洲人聚集的学校，以中国人、韩国人居多，而 CdM 恰恰相反，几乎看不到亚洲人。

我在网上调查并比较了两个学校的基本信息：DBHS 是 9 至 12 年级的 4 年高中，共有 3044 名学生，亚裔比例高达 64%，紧接着的拉丁裔占比 17%，而白人比例为 11%。这其中的亚裔大多为在美国出生长大的中国人和韩国人，但是近些年学校里的中国人比例猛增，坐着吃午饭都能听到隔壁的同学在说中文。CdM 是 7 至 12 年级的初中 + 高中，共有 2440 名学生，白人比例高达 82%，紧接着的亚裔占 9%，而拉丁裔占 6%。我们的学区其实有很多拉丁裔，但我们这个学校的拉丁裔学生非常少。我 10 年级刚转到 CdM 的时候，几乎看不到像我这样中国出生长大的学生，但我 11 年级开学的时候，发现中国人一下子多出来了！不出所料的话，学校的中国人比例将在今后几年逐步攀升，我也拭目以待。

从课程上来比较两所学校，我觉得是势均力敌的。每所学校都有不俗的 AP 课程（数量基本一致）及师资力量，但成绩好坏还是和任课老师息息相关。虽然在 DBHS 我只读了 9 年级，没有读 AP，但是通过高年级的朋友口中得出结论：完全看老师。有的老师教得好，有的老师根本不会教书，然后还会出很难的考试，所以无可奈何之下只好把 AP 课换掉。有的 AP 老师的教学还说得过去，考卷难度适中，虽然说 GPA 看上去很好，但是对 AP 考试拿 5 分满分并没有帮助。所以结论是，到美国读书——得靠自己，要想 AP 考试考得好并且学年成绩好的话有两个要素：上课认真听老师的讲课内容，跟着老师的思路及套路走，课后多提问；在考试前买课外辅导书，熟悉题型并且多练习真实考题，作为考前大复习。

　　不仅是 AP 课，在普通课程中也有好坏之分。同样一节 10 年级英语课，我 10 年级的英语老师是同学们心目中最棘手的（由于她是 12 年级 AP Literature 的老师），总爱让我们练写作然后放在投影仪上读。在她的课上拿 A 的概率极低，因为一不小心就栽在占比最大的写作上，然而写作机会少之又少，很难把分数抓上去。当然也有例外，我的好朋友两个学期都拿了 A。别的 10 年级老师就没有这么苛刻，批作文没有这么严格，考试形式也以选择题为主。虽然说这是一段"痛苦"的经历，对我来说也是一种磨炼。我经常鼓励我自己说：在未来的生活中并不知道还会碰到多少严苛挑剔的人，提前锻炼何曾不是一件好事？

说说体育和艺术——美国孩子们最爱的课后活动。从各种球类运动（棒球、橄榄球、足球、网球、曲棍球、篮球、排球等）到水上运动（游泳、水球），我见识了很多我从来不知道的运动。学校每年向大学输出许许多多的运动人才，他们最终的归属基本都是前20名的大学，大部分进了常春藤盟校的运动队。据我观察，很多孩子从小就开始专注于一项运动，通过十几年的历练达到了今天的成就，为了运动队也牺牲了很多时间。DBHS与CdM不同的是他们特别注重乐队和军乐队的培养，周末常常起个大早去比赛。为了拿到优异的名次，每天放学都要练上两个小时，所以军乐队相当于体育课。而CdM更爱的是各类体育运动和舞蹈，学校的啦啦队是姑娘们挤破头都想参加的活动（虽然也很辛苦，球队外出比赛都要一起出行），舞蹈队是全体学生的女神。在 DBHS，最有意思的是男子舞蹈队，也是全民男神，水平不是一般的高，在我看来他们在韩国出道是没什么问题的。

再来解说两个学校的课程时间安排。刚来美国读书的时候，我最不习惯的是每节课的时间太长了，要 1 个小时，初中在上海每节课才 40 分钟！而且课间休息还要跑不同的教室准备下一节课，没有时间和同学课间聊天。每天 6 节课，一周五天的课制按部就班，没有变化（私立学校会有不同的课程表，今天 A、明天 B）。每天早上 8 点准时上课，下午 3 点准时放学，老师从不拖堂，这对我来说感到新奇并且需要时间适应。到了新学校，第一年的课程表和 DBHS 一模一样，只是课时被拉长，午餐及课程休息时间被缩短。到了第二年，学校改成了 Block Schedule，一天上奇数的课表，一天上偶数的课表（每节课一个半小时，一天最多可以上 4 节课）。礼拜一是晚上学（Late Start），每节课都上。这是所有任课老师投票通过的，但是每节课每周就缩短了一个半小时。为了赶上进度，这些时间都潜移默化地加到作业上，尤其是 AP，因为进度受到推迟的话，在 5 月考试的时候会有很大损失。本来开学就比别的学校晚了半个月，在考试时将要累计损失高达 45 小时的课程时间！但在低年级及选修课老师看来，他们是双手赞同的，因为在原来的 6 节课基础上，同学们可以多修两门选修课，戏剧和唱歌都不会被耽误。

虽然说有些学校是有质的差距的。说到底，两个学校都有各自的好，不要将两个学校进行比较。我知道这是大家很感兴趣的一个话题，换学校不是一件容易的事。对我而言，在新学校的第一年很难，找不到好朋友，但是在适应了一段时间后就会感觉容易很多。交友是非常重要的一件事，当你有语言环境的时候——一定要找美国朋友！多练习才是口语提高的关键所在，不要想当然的和中国同学天天黏在一起，自己的英语没长进，朋友的英语也没长进，那到国外读书的意义又何在呢？在学校都不能好好适应社交生活的话，等工作后与外国同事的理念和隔阂便会越来越明显。显然，这不是如今中国父母拼了命也要送孩子出国念高中的意义。

DBHS VS CdM

All friends and family asked me if I like Diamond Bar High School（where I spent my freshman year）better or Corona del Mar High School better. I have to admit I love both of them. This was not the first time that I faced such question. It is the perfect analogy of what my relatives had asked me before many times，"Do you like your mom better or your dad better?" However, to answer this question I could say, the major difference between the schools is the ethnicity of the student body. DBHS is dominated by Asians, but CdM has predominantly a Caucasian student body.

I did research online to pull out some basic background information about both schools: DBHS is a 9 - 12 grades' 4 - year public high school, there are 3044 students for 2016 - 2017 school year. In terms of ethnicity, Asians is the majority of all ethnicities with 64% of Asian, 17% of Latino, and 11% of Caucasian background. Most of the Asians are ABC (American-born Chinese) /ABK (American-born Korean), but the percentage of Chinese students have increased rapidly in the recent years. I could hear Chinese being spoken all the time, everywhere on the campus. CdM is a 7 - 12 grades' middle and high school combination with 2440 students. 84% of the students are Caucasians, 9% of Asian, and 6% of Latino. My school district has a lot of Latinos, but there aren't a many in my school. When I transferred to CdM in sophomore year, I could merely see any Chinese, but I saw more Chinese and heard more Mandarin at the beginning of junior year. I believe there will be more incoming Chinese students in the years to come.

Both schools have strong academic programs, great AP programs, and experienced teachers. But your grade is greatly based on the teacher you get. Even though I didn't take any AP classes in DBHS, I heard a lot about the AP courses and classes: It all depends on the teacher. Some teachers have great teaching skills, some don't know how to teach and will give out difficult tests. Students have to drop the AP class in order to keep a good GPA. There are some teachers that are good teachers, easy graders, but they don't help with the AP exam at all. One thing I learned from school is that you need to help yourself out because no one will help you. In order to get an A in class and a perfect score on AP exam, you need to do the following: listen to teachers carefully in class and take notes when necessary. Try to be attentive and follow the teachers' line of thoughts. Don't forget to ask questions after class because questions are always welcomed. Buy test prep books at least 2 months before the exam to practice real tests and be well-prepared for the upcoming exams.

Not only the AP classes' level of difficulty depends on the instructors, even the regular classes have great differences. For example, my 10th grade English teacher is a tough grader (she is also the AP Literature teacher) who loves to give us writing assignments and read them under the document camera. It is extremely difficult to get an A in that class because if you get a bad grade on one of the writing assignments which weighs the most among all categories, it could drop the overall grade dramatically. Since there aren't many writing assignments, it is difficult to catch up later in the semester. There are high expectations that need to be meet. But other 10th grade English teachers were not as strict as mine was. Even though that was a painful experience, I learned a lot in that class and I elevated my writing to a high-end level.

I would like to mention sports and arts because these are Americans' favorite activities after school. From baseball, football, lacrosse, volleyball, football, golf, tennis, to swimming and water polo, I encountered many sports I haven't heard of before. Many athletes commit to the Top 20 universities in the nation, including Ivy League. They start early and dedicate to a specific sport from childhood and build up their skills over a decade to achieve the accomplishments. They sacrifice the precious weekends to go to games and practices. Compare to CdM, DBHS focuses on bands and music. DBHS's marching band goes to competitions almost every weekend during the competition season. In order to be placed in the top 3, the students have practice for 2 hours after school every weekday.

For arts, CdM has Orchesis and cheerleaders. A lot of girls want to participate in cheerleading program and everyone loves Orchesis girls! DBHS has all male dance teams which is unusual, but they are extremely good at dancing. They could qualify as "legit" KPOP stars.

When comparing two schools, one of the interesting core concepts to consider is the daily schedule. It takes time for me to adapt to the longer class period from a forty-minutes class I experienced in China to a sixty-minutes class in the U.S. I need to walk to different classrooms during passing period which differs from Chinese schools. There are 6 periods everyday, Monday through Friday. The schedule was almost the same when I transferred to CdM from DBHS, class starts at 8 AM and ends at 3 PM.

CdM changed to block schedule (longer periods) in 2016 – 2017 school year. There are odd block and even block. Every block is a solid 90 minutes class except Monday. Usually, we have odd periods on Tuesdays and Thursdays, and even periods on Wednesdays and Fridays. Monday is a late start day consists every class with shorter class periods. The staff members voted for the block schedule but such schedule causes us to lose 1.5 hours for each class every week. In order to compensate for the time loss according to this new schedule in the curriculum we would have a little more homework each night. It is bad especially for the AP classes because CdM starts in the beginning of September (which is 2 weeks behind other schools) and we will lose more than 45 hours of instructional time before the AP exams in May. But the block schedule is beneficial for other students who want to take multiple electives at the same time. They cannot do it in the regular 6 classes schedule but now students can choose up to 8 classes! Every student can choose 2 more classes than before.

I think it is unnecessary to compare two schools because both schools have pros and cons. Some schools think CdM is scandalous, but I like my school. It is not easy to transfer to a new school, and it is difficult to find good friends in a new environment. After a while, however, it becomes easier to find good friends. Finding the right friends and social groups is crucial for a student's educational development, especially for a foreign student. Stepping out of your comfort zone to communicate with American students can be very overwhelming. I truly advise foreign students to speak English while they are in the U.S. and speak less Mandarin. Practice is the key to become fluent English speakers. I encourage foreign students to expand their circle of friends by including native speakers. Hanging out with Chinese friends all day long won't help you with your English. At the end of the day, your English won't improve, neither will your friend's. What is the purpose of studying abroad if experiencing the culture and speaking the language are not on your list? If you can't adapt to the social life at school, the barrier between language and culture will become more difficult to overcome when you go to work. Apparently, this is not the intention of Chinese parents to spend all their wealth and energy to send their kids abroad at a young age.

CS，听说最近流行女孩学编程

Computer Science，编程，近年来备受追捧的 STEM，计算机科学成为了大热。全民学编程，我也是其中一个。从来没接触过编程，今年 9 月第一次开始学习 Java，从零开始。

先说说教课的老师，新泽西州长大，在高中时考了 AP Computer Science，高中考了 10 门 AP。今年 9 月（2016 年）开学前自学了半年 Java，成了我们的编程老师。考试题目的答案，他没有在程序里运行过，在评讲试卷的时候，被同学指出来他把题目批错了，他才发现问题。老师鼓励我们充分利用谷歌解答疑问，因为有些问题他也不懂。课上还有一位老师志愿者，是一名真正的程序员，利用他的空余时间来给我们上编程课，解答我们的疑问，在同学们的眼里他比真正的老师懂的多。由于课上的内容是把书上的内容全部搬到 PPT 上，考试前还是需要自己看书把内容吃透，不然考试云里雾里。

课上男女比例悬殊，32 人，25 位男生，7 位女生。课上有编程经验的人不超过 10 个。大部分人都是编程小白，在开学之前啥都不懂，得靠老师和同学的引导，才慢慢了解编程。我就是其中一个，零基础，全靠自己摸索。

我们现在上课用的书叫 *Building Java Programs: A back to basics Approach*（Third Edition），总共有 1146 页，18 个章节。开学三个多月，学习到第 7 章（跳过了第 6 章，大概是 AP 不考的内容），考了两次单元测试，即将进行第三次单元考试。这两个星期因为圣诞节的来临充斥着各门学科的考试（我们学校特别奇怪，是寒假结束之后进行期末考试），老师们都赶在放假之前帮我们巩固巩固知识，生怕 1 月份回来的时候把内容全都忘记了。

我开学时真没看出这本书会和 AP Computer Science 的考试有多大关系，有点担心我们学习的内容没有用，因此我特别去书店看了考试辅导书，发现内容还是很相似的，所以目前的教科书还是可以参考的。我喜欢现在这本教科书的原因是因为对于各个考点的解析很全面，而且有很多例子可以进行参考，这是考试辅导书不能提供的。

作业是编程课很重要的一方面，这里面包括基础的练习，也有将几个章节的内容综合起来的大项目。

我们平时的章节练习都是通过一个网站做的，叫 Practice it。这个网站把教科书上每个章节后的练习搬到了电脑上，把编码输进去后，网站会帮你执行编码并且找出编码中的错误。有时候题目很难根本做不出来，但是程序只会告诉你哪里有错误，而不会给提示，所以有时候做题目就会卡住。但幸好老师善解人意，说有偶尔的练习做不出来不要紧，只要能把大部分练习完成就可以了。（网址：http：//practiceit．cs．washington．edu/）

作为一门编程课，得擅长利用网络与谷歌。为了节约纸张及便利的缘故，我们所有的收交作业都是通过 Google Classroom 完成的。这是谷歌开发的一个网上教室，老师可以把作业的要求以及需要提交的内容全都发布在一个"教室"里，学生可以随时随地登录看当前需要提交的作业。编码用 txt 的方式递交，做的网上练习则用截屏的方式发给老师。老师还发现了一个新的网上教室，名叫 Repl．it，这是一个专门为编程课设计的网上教室，因为老师可以在这个平台上发布作业信息，并且学生可以在网站上写编码同时运行编码。老师说我们接下来的交作业平台会转移到 Repl，因为这省了他复制编码，再一个一个粘贴并运行的痛苦。

我觉得这个平台是所有编程课堂可以借鉴的，第一，这可以让学生随时随地写编码，没有时间地点的限制；第二，这节省了老师很多时间，检查作业速度可以提高很多。

写程序不可缺少的是编译器（Compiler），这是检验编码是否有效的程序。我们课上用的是 Eclipse，对于 Java 语言来说，这款编译器最好。如果编码中有问题，软件会跳出红色的×，点开会告诉你错误在哪里并且改正错误的几种方法。

当然，软件自带的内容解析是不够的，更多的时候需要谷歌。Stack Overflow 是我目前发现十分好用的一个编程交流平台（不只是 Java!），因为发布出来的编码都是 Java 的格式，一目了然。只要在 Google 上搜索疑问，Stack Overflow 的解析会出现在开头几条，点开可以看到完整的问题，决定与我问题的匹配度再看是否需要读下去。很多人的评论很专业，适合借鉴。

老师推荐我们用甲骨文（Oracle）自带的 Java 解析，但是我觉得信息量太大了，一个个看过来很费时间，还是要抓住重点，解决问题。

最后，推荐两个我这两年一直在关注的编程夏令营，而且这两个都是鼓励女孩子编程的非盈利组织。

① Girls Who Code（girlswhocode. com）：暑假夏令营长达 7 周，对暑假开学 11/12 年级的女孩开放，不收费，更有机会走进大型科技公司进行学习。每年收的人不多，所以我 2016 年申请没被录取。唯一的不好就是没有住宿，必须要有住家并且来回接送。

② Women's Technology Program（wtp. mit. edu）：MIT 举办的为期 4 周的夏令营，也是只对女生开放，因为美国近年来强烈呼吁女性加入科技行业，做一名光荣的程序猿。WTP 也是精英夏令营，收的人非常少。这个项目要求女生没有任何编程基础，完全

是从零开始的夏令营。像我这种在学计算机科学的人，这个项目就不会收了。WTP对于申请者的要求比较高，需要读美高的同学才能申请。具体的还是请到官网上详细阅读。

文章最后我要唠叨几句，编程并不是适合每一个人的。有些人觉得编程很有意思，热衷于写编码，然而也有一大部分人对编程一点都不感兴趣，这完全因人而异。不要认为编程是近年来的大热，就一定要跟风学编程，我认为是完全没有必要的。因为每个人的兴趣爱好都不一样。对我而言，我喜欢高科技，也想系统地学习编程，我非常幸运有这个机会，所以我要抓住机会。我认为这个世界的未来是科技和网络，因此我选择了这门课。

但我还是鼓励大家尝试，引用习近平主席的一句话："鞋子合不合脚，自己穿了才知道。"

Computer Science, girls who code is the new trend

Computer Science (aka coding), as STEM is gaining more attention and popularity in the recent years, has become one of the hottest topics. Everyone wants to take a coding class, that included me. I had never learned coding before but had always wanted to. Starting the fall of junior year, I started to learn Java which I had no knowledge of.

Having a good and knowledgeable Computer Science teacher is crucial to a student's success in this AP Class. My teacher grew up in New Jersey. He took AP Computer Science test in high school . He learned Java 6 months before the fall semester of 2016 and became my school's new AP Computer Science teacher. He strongly encourages the students to collaborate and search for solutions on Google in

23

order to succeed in the course because there are so much contents in Java and he might not be able to demonstrate them all.

Occasionally, there will be a teacher volunteer who is a real coder in life to give out lectures and answer our questions. Everyone loves him because not only is he a good teacher, he also knows how to link the projects to real life situations. He always brings useful information and teaches the way how the industry utilizes coding. Since the lectures overlap textbook, reading and studying the textbook are essential.

The gender ratio in the class is extremely unbalanced: there are 32 students in the class, among which 25 of the students are boys, and only 7 of them are girls. In that class, fewer than 10 students have coding experience. Most students' knowledge of coding before that class was next to zero. I was one of those students who had no previous understanding of coding. We use a fundamental textbook called:

Building Java Programs: A back to basics Approach (*Third Edition*). This book contains 18 chapters, 1146 pages in total. Three months into the first semester, we had two unit tests and studied 7 chapters. The teacher keeps reviewing the material with us everyday because he is afraid that students will forget the useful contents and coding is all about cumulative knowledge.

As the second semester starts and the AP exam approaches, the teacher becomes stricter on quizzes. Starting February, we have an AP style free response quiz every week. The frequency increases by one quiz every month till AP exam which is the second day of AP Exams.

At the beginning of the school year, I didn't know how the AP test works and thought the textbook's content would not appear on the exam. I was worried therefore I went to Barnes & Nobles to verify the AP test prep book. The contents on the prep books parallel our textbook then I felt relieved and believed that I was on the right track.

Assignment is an imperative part of computer science. It includes basic reading and practices and there are also challenging projects combining skills from multiple chapters.

We did the basic chapter practices online through a website called 'Practice it'. The website copied all the self-check questions at the end of each chapter in the textbook. 'Practice it' runs and compiles the codes for you and gives you feedback when there are errors in the code. The biggest struggle I faced with 'Practice it' was that it indicated there were errors but never specified how to modify the program to make it compile and run correctly. Luckily, my teacher was flexible on the practice as long as I finished the majority of practices.

Due to the complicated nature of coding, it is impossible to know all the codes by heart. Utilizing technology and Google are some of the essential aspects in managing the enormous amount of codes.

All of our assignments are posted on Google Classroom. At the beginning of the semester, all of the codes were submitted as text (txt). This was not the most efficient method for our teacher to check every student's homework because he needed to copy every single assignment into the compiler and run it manually. Our teacher discovered a new online compiler called 'Repl. it' which is unfathomably convenient and time efficient. It is an online coding "Google Classroom" because our teacher can post all the information and details of assignments on there and we would simply submit the codes after. After using it for a few months, I recognized what the benefits and weaknesses of the online compiler are. It is user friendly because it is web-based, this means you can access the code anywhere without installing an actual compiler. Second, the teacher can put all the information next to the code that I don't need to flip between the document and compiler. But the disadvantage of online compiler is obvious: there are fewer features due to the memory space. Similar to 'Practice it', 'Repl. it' can not provide specific options to modify the code. But the traditional compiler can provide detailed information about the errors and multiple alternatives to solve the problem.

Using a compiler in coding is vital because it checks and runs programs. The compiler I use in class is Eclipse, it is the first choice for Java coders. What I enjoy about this software is that it gives notifications when errors occur in the program, then simply by clicking on the designated mark will provide specific solutions to solve the problem.

Of course, the compiler is not everything. Use Google for research is helpful because teacher won't be able to solve all the questions. When there are difficult questions, Google would be your best friend. The best website I have yet encountered is 'Stack Overflow', it is an online computer science community with millions of adept coders who are able to answer the questions. The answers are in Java format, so it is easy to read and copy into the compiler and run it. The most meticulous answers would usually be on the top of the page. If you realize their solutions don't match your question, then find another post and read it. I highly recommend reading posts on 'Stack Overflow' because you can find most of the answers on there.

Besides Stack Overflow, teacher recommends Oracle's Java analysis but I found that there was unnecessary information and it became boring and overwhelming after reading for a while. It was difficult to extract the useful information but I would recommend that one read it if he or she wants to learn Java thoroughly with every small detail.

Finally, I would like to recommend two summer programs for coding that I have eyed for quite some time. Both of them encourage girls to code and both of them are nonprofit organizations. They don't accept any girls who had taken AP Computer Science before or have any prior knowledge about computer science.

① Girls Who Code (girlswhocode. com): The summer immersion program lasts for 7 weeks and is open for rising Junior and Senior girls. The program is free. All the girls get to have sessions in high tech corporations and they have great technology influencers who come to the girls to inform them about the technology industry. They accept a small number of students coming from different areas of the U.S. The disadvantage of the program is that instead of a residential program, it is a commuter one. Unfortunately, no dorms are provided.

② Women's Technology Program (wtp. mit. edu): Yes, it takes place in MIT. The program lasts for 4 weeks; similar to Girls Who Code, it is only open for girls as the industry is calling for more females to join the STEM family. The program only accepts around 40 girls every year therefore the chance of getting admitted is slim to nails. The program requires girls who have held no computer science background and should be current high school juniors in the U.S. For more details, please visit their site.

After all, I have to conclude my feelings about AP Computer Science and the STEM industry as a whole. Some people think coding is interesting and they are passionate about it, but the vast majority has no interest in computer science. They take the class just because it is an AP course and STEM is the hottest topic that leads to great job opportunities and a bright future. Don't take a coding class if you are not passionate about it. Don't ever follow others' steps blindly which could lead to regrettable decisions as well as failing your dreams. For me personally, I love technology and I would love to learn computer science thoroughly. Luckily, I am good at it and I will be forever grateful for the opportunity I had. I believe the future is all about technology and the Internet, therefore I chose this class.

Like President Xi's saying, "You don't know if

the shoes fit unless you try them on." Even though I encourage everyone to try, don't push yourself too hard.

AP 英语，我恨你，我爱你

11 年级和 12 年级的 AP 英语叫法不同，学的东西也不一样。11 年级的叫 AP Language and Composition，以写作为主，12 年级的叫 AP Literature and Composition，以阅读文学作品为重点，都是世界名著。

因为很多学生都选了这门课，所以学校共有两位 11 年级的 AP 英语老师。她们在暑假里就会制定好一整年的学习方案（很多 AP 老师都这么做，为了保证进度），还把我们的文件夹分成了六种颜色，每种颜色都是不一样的类别，为了方便分类，老师用的打印纸是和分类隔层的颜色一致的。

6 大板块分别为：选择题（Multiple Choice）、基本要素/重要内容（Nuts and Bolts）、修辞解析（Rhetorical Analysis）、议

论文（Argument）、综合写作（Synthesis）、文学（Novel/Literature）。

今年的英语老师和我们说，AP Language 的写作和阅读很多都是和当今社会有关的。与 12 年级的 AP Literature 不同，因为 Literature 学习的古典文学与当今社会是脱节的。所以我们老师给我们阅读的文章很多都是很有争议性的话题，包括 2016 年戏剧化的美国大选，这也是我们课堂里聪明孩子们热衷讨论的话题。课上的文章讨论，转眼间就变成了一场辩论赛。

英语课的成绩划分如下：作业：15%；诚信分（Integrity）：5%；课堂讨论/小组项目：10%；测验：30%；写作：40%。

作为英语课，课堂重心当然还是写作和阅读。暑假加上第一学期，一共读了 5 本书，而且这些书老师都是让我们课后在家自行阅读，为了不占用课堂时间阅读其他的各类文章。

书评：

① *Sin and Syntax——How to craft wicked good prose*（《语法与罪恶——如何写出一流的散文》）：这本是暑假作业，作为一门以写作为主的英语课，语法是很重要的一部分。如何生动地使用动词、名词、形容词，如何使用不同的句式来使文章更加有趣。作者试图用更加生动的例子来吸引读者的注意力，因为说到底这还是一本枯燥的语法书。老师给我们讲课的时候，会帮我们划重点，因为这本书生词多，而且她知道我们肯定懒得认真读。课后会把章节最后的题目留给我们当回家作业。

② *The Crucible*（《萨勒姆的女巫》）：一个剧本，也是我们的暑假作业。我觉得内容还是挺有趣的，值得读一下。这本书也是在美国历史上的一本经典名作，讲述了普通人在威胁和恐惧中的勇敢和谎言。老师给我们讲了一下这本书的创作及历史背景，开学第

一周直接布置与书内容相关的作文作业，并且把这篇文章算在写作分类里。作为总分的40%，一开学同学们的成绩就一落千丈，包括我。

③ *Into the wild*（《荒野生存》）：一位真名叫 Chris McCandless 的 Emory 大学高材生在大学毕业后背井离乡，把积攒下来的钱全都捐了出去，然后一个人用自己新创的名字探险阿拉斯加的真人故事。这是作者 Jon Krakauer 在采访与 Chris 有过交集的人后写下的非小说散文。这本书背后讲述的是人性、自由与超越论（transcendentalism）。刚开始看的时候会感觉很无聊，但是故事越到后面越有趣，会忍不住看下去。因为我整个人被故事情节吸引了，所以看的速度也会快起来。同学和我说这本书翻拍的电影也不错，有兴趣可以去看一下。

④ *The Awakening*（《觉醒》）：这是一个住在新奥尔良州的一名家庭妇女 Edna 在家庭

海边度假的时候学会了游泳，她在尝试了自己从来不敢做的事情后，开始寻找离开家庭及逃避日常繁琐事务的机会，寻找爱情并且获得"重生"的故事。Edna 的行为对于保守的南部来说是不可理喻的，所以这也是一本十分具有争议的小说。整个故事围绕着女权展开，开放式的结局把答案留给了观众。不同的角度看到的结局是不同的，她到底是获得了重生，还是接受了命运的审判？

⑤ *The Great Gatsby*：这本书也不需要我多介绍了，因为这是人尽皆知的《了不起的盖茨比》。好几年前看的电影，情节都忘得差不多了。这本书给我的感觉也是开始读会觉得很没劲，但是越读到后面越有意思，也是停不下来。

测评形式：

我们平时的小测验和考试非常少，基本以写作及课堂讨论为主。唯一的考试就是期末考试，其他的测评都通过小组项目或课堂讨论完成。

① Socratic Seminar（问答讨论会），一整个班级的同学围成一个圈，一半的同学坐在内圈，一半的同学坐在外圈。老师会在讨论前一个星期让我们准备（Prep work），这里面都是有关于文章写作手法以及中心思想的问题，需要我们在文中找到直接的句子论证观点。最后将答案以段落形式打印出来，作为分数的一部分。最重要的就是 Socratic Seminar，讨论部分。说起来，就是优雅的辩论。不需要举手发言，想说就说，但是不能两个人同时说。因为每个人对于同一件事物的看法是不一样的，所以这种活动是一个很好的交流平台。讨论中会碰撞出新的火花，对我来说也是一个很好的学习机会。老师还会计算每个人发言的次数，没达到一定次数，还会扣分。*Into the Wild* 和 *The Awakening* 都是通过全班讨论的方式结束的。

② Sketch Flection（概述部分），看一章

节，从中心思想、写作手法或是老师指定的特殊视角（Critical Lens）出发，写一段文章并且配上图片，阐述自己对每个章节的理解，最后将所有的文章汇总起来做成一本小册子。解释一下 Critical Lens 是什么。老师给每个同学分配了不同的视角，通过一个特殊的视角去阅读这本小说。这其中包括女权主义（Feminism）、马克思主义/政治（Marxist）、读者读后感（Reader Response），每个角度都有不同的重点。

写作：

重中之重，我一直在强调写作很难，但是很重要。AP Language 考试一共要写三篇文章，一篇解读文章修辞手法（Rhetorical Analysis），一篇通过阅读 6 篇材料树立个人观点的综合文章（Synthesis Essay），还有一篇是议论文（Argument）。修辞手法（Rhetorical Analysis）和综合文章（Synthesis Essay），老师都是有套路的。

老师首先会让我们做与文章类型相关的小组活动，这样可以对文章及题材有一个大概的了解。接着就会发各类文章与写作指南，把文章的整体框架及写作需要注意的事项及要点全都罗列出来。

在正式写作前，老师会让我们读 3 篇大学委员会（College Board）发出来的模板文章（Anchor Paper），每篇文章的水平参差不齐，老师通过小组形式让同学们对每篇文章进行评分及点评，最后总结出好的文章和差的文章的区别，为了给接下来的当堂计时写作做铺垫。

老师会让我们写两次文章，把自己感觉写得更好的一篇文章给她，然后她通过 AP 英语的写作打分表（9 分制，9 分为满分）来打分，算入写作成绩。这就像赌博，你永远不知道你选的那篇到底是写得好的，还是写得差的。

我得岔开讲一下如何提高议论文的写

作，因为这和综合性文章及修辞手法不太一样。老师给我们布置了一项长达一个月的项目，名叫"追踪专栏作家"（"Following a Columnist"）。"追踪专栏作家"和议论文也息息相关。AP 考试中的议论文只给一个命题，不像综合写作会给 5～6 篇补充文章做参考，让同学提出个人观点。议论文完全是凭借个人的生活阅历及知识素养来写的。

给大家打个比方，这个命题是我在课堂上写的：

Consider the distinct perspectives expressed in the following statements.

If you develop the absolute sense of certainty that powerful beliefs provide, then you can get yourself to accomplish virtually anything, including those things that other people are certain are impossible.

William Lyon Phelps, *American educator*, *journalist*, *and professor* （1865 – 1943）

I think we ought always to entertain our opinions with some measure of doubt. I shouldn't wish people dogmatically to believe any philosophy, not even mine.

Bertrand Russell, British author, mathematician, and philosopher (1872 – 1970)

In a well-organized essay, take a position on the relationship between certainty and doubt. Support your argument with appropriate evidence and examples.

通过两句名人的引语来引出文章命题。William 认为必然性（Certainty）是最重要的，必然性可以使人们实现所有的梦想，甚至那些旁人无法想象的梦想。而 Bertrand 完全不赞同这个看法，他认为有质疑精神（Doubt）才是最重要的品质，不能教条式地相信某一个的观点或信仰，甚至不要完全相信他说的话。最后一小节引出了文章命题：在一篇组织有序的文章中，表达自己对于必然性与质疑关系的观点，使用适当的证据来证明自己的观点。

如果你需要在 40 分钟内写出这篇作文（字数不限），你有什么观点和想法吗？用什么例子和历史事件来证实自己的观点？能在 40 分钟内构思并且完成吗？议论文每次的问题都很抽象，要多读几遍命题，理清思路，才能开始写。

为了让同学们拓宽视野，英语老师给同学们布置了一个大项目——跟踪专栏作家。老师给同学们提供了一系列鼎鼎有名的专栏作家，有兴趣的可以（翻墙）关注一下，看一下有没有自己喜欢的文章。大多都和政治有关，我还挺关心政治的，若是没兴趣也不必强行去读。因为这是持续一个月的项目，所以老师希望我们找的专栏作家是经常更新的，以保证新闻及时有效。在老师给的一系列作家中，我去读了他们的专栏，结果有的文章写得太长，有的文章停很久或者隔一长段时间才更新，所以我最终选择了《时代周刊》（TIME）杂志的北京特派记者 Charlie Campbell。

他的写作风趣幽默，长度适中，难度并不高，所以我觉得有兴趣的朋友可以去读读他写的文章。我爱上他文章的原因是我读了他写了一篇关于中国雾霾的文章：*Chinese People Are Buying All Kinds of Desperate Remedies to Protect Themselves From Smog*（《中国人民正在购买五花八门的绝望补救用具来拯救生活在雾霾中的自己》）。

选三个章节给大家解读一下 Campbell 是如何通过事实（Fact）、解读（Value）以及解决方案（Policy）来论证他的个人观点。

Following a welcome burst of blue skies over Lunar New Year, chronic smog returned to northern China this week, prompting the wearing of face masks and the switching on of air purifiers as airborne particle levels soared to

10 times WHO safe levels.

中国春节的蓝天过后，常年不息的雾霾在本周继续笼罩中国北方，人们在空气污染指数高达世界卫生组织（World Health Organization）的安全标准 10 倍之时，立即戴起了口罩，打开了空气净化器。这是文章的第一小节，通过将北方的空气污染指数与世界卫生组织的数据进行对比，强调污染的严重性。通过"returned"这个词，说明了这是常态，春节期间的蓝天是个别现象。

Boasting ingredients such as "polygonatum，kumquat，lily，red dates，chrysanthemum and rock candy," the latter are claimed by manufacturers to "alleviate the harm to the human body of long-term inhalation of air pollution." Traditional Chinese Medicine (TCM) practitioners are unimpressed，though；Liu Quanqing, president of the Beijing Hospital of TCM，told China's state media last month that such concoctions were "unreliable" and "may cause health problems if taken for a long time."

进补药材，包括玉竹、金桔、百合、红枣、菊花以及冰糖，都被制造商称为具有"减缓人体长期呼吸雾霾空气所带来的伤害"的功效。但是传统中医并不对厂商的推销手段感冒，北京中医医院院长刘泉清通过媒体告诉大众这样的调制品是"不可靠的"并且"若长期使用有可能对人体造成危害"。在陈述中国空气质量现状后，Campbell 引出了文章的重点——人们如何用形形色色的补救方法在雾霾中保护自己。这一小节通过商家的销售手段以及中医医师对其商品功效的不屑一顾来证明我们所做的这一切都是无用功。通过直接引用中医的话来加强论点的说服力，以及这些药补潜在的危害。

Xiaomi should know what it's talking about. Late last month, global vice president Hugo Barra quit the Beijing-based firm to

move back to California，saying that "the last
few years of living in such a singular
environment have taken a huge toll on my life
and started affecting my health."

　　小米对于雾霾的危害再清楚不过了。上
个月（2017 年 1 月），小米的全球副总裁
Hugo Berra 辞去了在北京工作的机会，搬回
了加州。Berra 说："过去几年生活在北京单
一的环境中对我的人生敲响了警钟并且严重
地影响了我的身体健康"。Campbell 继续沿
用他擅长的举例子，用小米全球副总裁，有
权威性的例子，来证明雾霾正在将人"赶
走"。Campbell 在文章最后并没有写实际的
解决措施，因为在他看来现在都没有实效的
补救方案，我们还是在自我安慰。

　　除了这些，还有课堂上做的、读的那些
文章：

　　——Multiple Choice Monday（周一多项
选择题）：与写作并称两大恶魔，老师从不同

的 AP 辅导书及历届考题抽取阅读文章，每篇的选择题数量在 10～15 个之间。文章有几道题，老师就给几分钟看文章＋完成选择题。

选择题是噩梦的原因：很多时候，文章内容很深，不容易理解。第二，答案很相近，模棱两可的时候就会选错。第三，修辞手法题总会出现不认识的生词，都是以前没看到过的修辞手法，例如，Anaphora（首语重复法）、Asyndeton（连接词省略）、Polysyndeton（连词叠用）、Epistrophe（尾词重复）。当这些词长得很像，但是意思相反的时候，只能靠第六感——蒙题。

当然，如果你这些词都会了，而且可以在写作中灵活运用，你就离 AP 考试拿 5 分又近了一步。

——读形形色色的文章：我们读过亚里士多德的著作 *The aim of man*，告诉我们快乐至上，一篇 20 页的文章重复地在强调一个点；杰弗逊的独立宣言 *Declaration of Independence*；

也读过发表在杂志 The New Yorker 上的现代文章 *What is a woman*，讲述了变性人在当下的生存状况等文章。（题外话：于是，英语老师把生物老师省下来的纸，全都用完了……）

老师一直和我们强调要在文章上做批注、划重点，写下自己的想法，这对做练习题及写作时很有帮助，因为这样才能更快地抓重点，完成题目。

这只是课堂的一小部分，课上阅读很多和历史有关的文章都和美国独立及历史发展有着紧密的联系，所以我发现英语课上读的内容和历史课是交相辉映的。某一天老师在历史课上讲女性在 20 世纪争取投票权的话题，突然英语老师就布置给我们一篇关于女权的文章。英语比历史更加复杂，因为除了论述事实，英语课上还要讨论并解析作者的写作手法及效果，作者陈述的个人立场，以及作者口吻。

如果你问我读这些书对考 AP 有帮助吗，我会回答有或者没有。

读书的目的不是仅仅为了考试，而是为了培养批判性思维，树立正确的世界观，以及拓展课外知识，书中的故事是学校里不能教会你的。读书中穿插的活动与练习对于 AP 考试是绝对有帮助的，因为读得越多，阅读速度就会越快，在写作分析的时候也可以解析得更透彻。我写的文章老师一直和我说，引用的句子太长了，然而解析的内容就只有一两行，要 DM（Develop More），将整个句子吃透，把内容拓展开。

但是这些书的内容不一定会出现在 AP 考试中，所有的阅读都是为了 AP 考试做铺垫。不代表你读并且彻底理解了这些书，AP 就可以考满分了，根本不存在这种逻辑。

希望大家在读完这篇文章后，对于 AP Language and Composition 可以有好的了解，但是读不读是你的事。

你问我读得开心吗？我告诉你，痛苦并快乐着。

My love and hate relationship with AP English

Junior and Senior's AP English have different names. Junior's AP English is called "AP English Language and Composition", which focuses on writing. Senior's AP English is labeled "AP Literature and Composition", which emphasizes reading world-known literature.

There are 2 AP English Language teachers because the majority of juniors enroll in this class. Teachers came together and planned the first semester's schedule during summer (a lot of AP teachers like to plan ahead to keep up the pace) and they even sort all the documents into 6 different colors. Each color is a different category and the paper related to a certain category will be printed in the specific colored paper to match the binder dividers.

These six categories include: Multiple Choice, Nuts and Bolts, Rhetorical Analysis, Argument, Synthesis, Novel/Literature.

My English teacher is Mrs. Yennie. She is one of the sweetest people I have ever known. She told us the difference between AP Language and AP Literature on the first day. AP Language is all about the society today, on the other hand, the reading and writing all build around the society. Majority of the articles we read are controversial, including the dramatic 2016 President election year——one of the hottest topics for all the (politics-driven) smarties in class. Sometimes a basic article discussion would turn into a hot debate immediately. Dialectic is an extremely beneficial method for individuals to not only engage in each other's thoughts but also to challenge one another's view on reality. One can learn and broaden his or her horizon about any topic in the world through productive discussions.

The weighting of English class is as follow:

Integrity: 5%; Homework: 15%; Socratic Seminar/ Project: 10%; Tests/Quizzes: 30%; Writing: 40%.

As an English Class, writing and reading are still the main focus. We read five books during the summer and the first semester. Most of the time the reading is done at home for the sake of limited time in class. Here is a brief description about each book:

① *Sin and Syntax——How to Craft wicked good prose*: This was one of the summer assignments that concentrates on grammar and syntax since the emphasis of AP Language class is writing. A few essential skills we learned in class were: how to use nouns, verbs, adjectives effectively; how to utilize different sentence structures to make the essay more appealing; and finally, how to express our feelings by instigating our inner creativity to form a soul grasping essay that would resonate with readers. Although the author tries to use vivid examples to enthrall readers, it is still an educational and dry grammar book. Mrs. Yennie would highlight the key points of each chapter for us and leave a little writing assignment at the end of class.

② *The Crucible* : A fiction story about Salem's witchcraft took place in the 17th century and it was also one of the summer readings. Personally, I love the book and I recommend that everyone reads this magnificent book at some point in life. This book is also a classic one which teaches a great lesson on different people's bravery and fear when witchcraft rumors were spread across the city. Mrs. Yennie assigned us to compose an essay about the book during the first week of school. Nearly all students experienced a dramatic curve because writing is 40% of the overall grade and I was one of the victims, too.

③ *Into the Wild* : An Emory College undergrad Chris McCandless left the school, donated all his money, and lived a new life using a completely different name. This nonfiction book was written by Jon Krakauer after he followed the steps of Chris McCandless on his way to Alaska and interviewed the people Chris encountered on his journey. The book is about freedom, personality, and transcendentalism. The story proceeds slowly in the beginning, but it becomes more interesting and intriguing as it goes on. Personally, I loved the plot and the suspension of the story. It was a quick read for me. My friends tell me that the movie based on *Into the Wild* is also a good one. I would recommend everyone to take some time and watch it then decide whether to read the book or not.

④ *The Awakening*: Edna, a housewife in New Orleans, learned how to swim during her annual family summer vacation. After that, she found herself capable of doing many things she had never tried before. She avoided the daily chores, left the house, found her true love besides her husband, and reborn. Edna was not widely accepted in the conservative South which makes this novel a controversial one. The story builds around feminism, and Chopin left the ending open for the readers to come to their own conclusion. Has she reached mental/ emotional awaking? Does she die under god's power?

⑤ *The Great Gatsby*: This book is a must read for all high school students in the U.S. The movie that came out a few years ago was fantastic, but I forgot most of the plot. Therefore, the reading was a great recap for me. The love and hate relationship between characters, desire for wealth, and the pursue of the ultimate American Dream are worth noticing and pondering on. If you had never read it before, you should do so within near future.

There are not many tests and quizzes throughout the semester except the 'Multiple Choice Monday'. The overall score is mostly built up by writing and discussion.

① Socratic Seminar: The whole class put the desks into a circle, half of the students sit in the inner circle and the other half sit in the outer circle. Mrs. Yennie would usually hand out the prep work one week prior to the discussion with free response questions about the rhetorical devices that the author utilizes and the theme of the whole book. The answers should include specific quotes in the book and print out the short answers as a portion of the overall grade. The Socratic Seminar discussion portion is beneficial. It is an elegant debate without raising hands. You can speak at any time when no one else is speaking. It is a great learning opportunity because I get to hear different classmates' responses to the same question from various perspectives. Mrs. Yennie would also record how many times you have spoken to give you a final grade.

② Sketch Flection: After reading every chapter, we would write a short passage based on Mrs. Yennie's assigned critical lens. Further, we would add details and pictures to express one's comprehension on the chapter and assemble the pages together to create a journal. For a quick explanation of critical lenses, Mrs. Yennie assigned each student a different lens and let them read the chapter from the specific perspective. For *The Great Gatsby*, it includes feminism, Marxism, and reader response. Each lens has a different emphasis.

Writing:

The most important category of all. I always emphasize the difficulty of writing, but it is the crucial part of AP Language exam because the exam consists three essays: Rhetorical Analysis, Synthesis Essay, and Argument Essay. All of them have a basic format to follow.

Before the actual writing, Mrs. Yennie would put us into groups to discuss the general information of each type of essay and give us handouts on the essay's structure and key points to succeed in the writing. She would also let us read the anchor paper published by College Board and let us critique and grade them. By comparing and contrasting the anchor papers, we became ready for the actual Timed Write. Such foundations assist us in developing and tackling any possible issues one might face.

Mrs. Yennie would have us write two essays with different prompts and allowed us to choose the one we preferred. She would then grade it according to the AP rubric (9 is the highest grade one can obtain) and the grade counts as part of the writing category in the gradebook. Handing 1 of the 2 essays is like gambling because you will never know if the one you choose is the well-written one or not.

I have to digress a little to talk about argument essay because it is different from rhetorical analysis or synthesis. Argument essays require the writer to have a broad range of knowledge in order to write about it. Mrs. Yennie assigned a project called "Following a columnist" that lasts for one month which will broaden our knowledge. Every student needs to find and follow a columnist for a month. When the students find the articles they like, they can print them out and annotate them. This project will help us to persuade the readers in the essay because we get to learn more facts in this project.

Here is an actual AP exam argument prompt we used in class:

Consider the distinct perspectives expressed in the following statements.

If you develop the absolute sense of certainty that powerful beliefs provide, then you can get yourself to accomplish virtually anything, including those things that other people are certain are impossible.

William Lyon Phelps, *American educator*, *journalist*, *and professor* (1865 – 1943)

I think we ought always to entertain our opinions with some measure of doubt. I shouldn't wish people dogmatically to believe any philosophy, not even mine.

Bertrand Russell, *British author*, *mathematician*, *and philosopher* (1872 – 1970)

In a well-organized essay, take a position on the relationship between certainty and doubt. Support your argument with appropriate evidence and examples.

While William believed that certainty can help people to accomplish anything in life even when everyone else disagree, Bertrand believed that doubt is the greatest quality because no one should follow a dogmatic belief or idea, not even his words. In the last paragraph, the prompt asked the students to write a well-organized essay that examines the relationship between doubt and certainty, use appropriate evidence to support their arguments. If you only have 40 minutes to write this essay, what are you going to write? Can you organize a well-written essay in less than 40 minutes? All argument essays' prompts are rather abstract, which require the students to read the prompt multiple times before they start to write.

Since "Following a Columnist" lasts for a month, Mrs. Yennie wants us to find a writer that publishes articles often to make sure the information is up to date. I chose the Beijing correspondent for TIME, Charlie Campbell. His articles are fun and moderate in length and difficulty, I recommend his column if you are interested in world politics. I was in loved with his writing when I read his article about China's air pollution titled *Chinese People Are Buying All Kinds of Desperate Remedies to Protect Themselves From Smog*.

Here are some short excerpts from the article to demonstrate how Campbell uses fact, value, and policy to argue his claim.

"Following a welcome burst of blue skies over Lunar New Year, chronic smog returned to northern China this week, prompting the wearing of face masks and the switching on of air purifiers as airborne particle levels soared to 10 times WHO safe levels."

The opening paragraph creates a strong comparison between the standard airborne particle level to northern China's. The word "returned" emphasizes that it is the common state of northern China during winter time. The fact makes Campbell's argument valid and persuasive.

"Boasting ingredients such as ' polygonatum,

kumquat, lily, red dates, chrysanthemum and rock candy,' the latter are claimed by manufacturers to 'alleviate the harm to the human body of long-term inhalation of air pollution.' Traditional Chinese Medicine (TCM) practitioners are unimpressed, though; Liu Quanqing, president of the Beijing Hospital of TCM, told China's state media last month that such concoctions were 'unreliable' and 'may cause health problems if taken for a long time.' "

Campbell points out the value of the column by citing expert's quotes to argue the desperate remedies Chinese are using to protect themselves in extreme weather are not as glamorous as they sound. Campbell appeals to ethos by using the prestigious practitioner's quotes to claim that these boasting ingredients are useless and potentially harmful.

"Xiaomi should know what it's talking about. Late last month, global vice president Hugo Barra quit the Beijing-based firm to move back to

California, saying that 'the last few years of living in such a singular environment have taken a huge toll on my life and started affecting my health.' "

To end the article, Campbell brings in another fact that Xiaomi's (the leading technology corporation in China) vice president resigned because he could not endure the weather anymore. Campbell doesn't provide any policy to fight the smog in northern China and he leaves the answer open. From his perspective, he cannot think of any sufficient solutions to the smog crisis. Chinese are just consoling themselves. Feel free to read the full article on TIME's website or visit my official account in WECHAT (Search and add BettyTheScientist in the official account tab).

Reading in class, yes, we read a lot:

① Multiple Choice Monday: same level of evilness comparing to Timed Write. Mrs. Yennie usually pulls out passages from different AP English prep books or from the past AP exams. Every passage has between 10 − 15 questions. The number of questions determines the minutes Mrs. Yennie would give. If there are 10 questions in the passage, you would be given 10 minutes to read and answer the 10 multiple choice questions. Multiple Choice Monday is a nightmare because the passages are very in depth, full of details that would make it impossible to recall. Second, the answer choices are so similar which makes it difficult to pick the right answer even if you narrow it down to 2 answer choices. Third, I have to deal with vocabulary and rhetorical devices that I had never seen before. For example, anaphora, asyndeton, polysyndeton, epistrophe. When they look identical but have opposite meanings, common sense would be the only option left.

Of course, if you master all the vocabulary and develop strong analytic skills, you are one step closer to obtaining a 5 on the actual exam.

② various readings: From Aristotle's *The Aim of man*, which stresses the pursue of happiness for 20 pages, to Thomas Jefferson's *Declaration of Independence*, are only a fraction of the intriguing readings we did. The readings did not only shed light on historical treasures, we also had a great taste of contemporary articles, such as *What is a woman* that describes the real life of a transgender in New York City. (therefore the English teachers use all the paper that Biology teachers try to save)

Mrs. Yennie emphasizes the importance of highlighting quotes, annotating along the way, and writing down side notes when reading. These strategies will help a lot in writing and reading because you can find the central idea and the author's claim more easily.

This is only a portion of the class, as the time progresses, I realize that a great number of articles we covered in class are related to U.S. History. We learned about social issues such as independence, African Americans' struggles in the American society, and women's rights in depth. One day my history teacher was talking about the women's suffrage in the 20th century, and a few days later Mrs. Yennie assigned a reading about the suffrage right in the 1920s. English is more complicated than regular U.S. History because we need to analyze the author's rhetorical strategies and effects besides the rudimentary facts.

When asked if the readings we did in class contribute to a high AP score, I would claim both yes and no.

Reading and discussion are not solely for the test, but more importantly they are for practicing critical thinking, building a personal value, and broadening one's knowledge. These are all the great aspects of AP Language and Composition. There are countless life lessons in the books that one will not merely learn by attending lectures alone no matter how attentive one is. Reading activities and practices are helpful for the exam without a doubt because when you read more, you will be able to read faster and analyze better. I used to implement long quotes in my essays, however, I was not truly capable of meticulously analyzing the quotes. Mrs. Yennie always gave productive feedback when I had this specific problem in writing. Analyzing quotes accurately and effectively is something I am practicing today and will use for my future essays.

Even though these books won't be included in the AP exam, they are all the building blocks for the AP exam in May. It is not true that simply by reading the books in class and comprehending the concepts would lead to a 5 on the exam.

I hope my explanation would help you understand AP Language and Composition better but the decision of taking the test or not is your choice.

If you ask me whether I love the class or not, let me tell you, I hate it but I love it even more.

学校的领袖组织徒有其名？

美国学校特别注重领导力，所以学校里有各种各样的领袖组织（Leadership group）。在我 9 年级的学校，除了学校的学生会（Assistant Student Body）是需要选拔的之外，其他的所谓"领导力"社团都只是学生自行组织的，没有选拔一说，都是只要报名就能参加。

CdM 有 5 个领导力社团，都是需要面试/选拔决定最终人选的：

• ASB（Assistant Student Body）：5 个领导力社团里，我认为气氛最嗨的一个。社团里的每一个人都特别会玩。ASB 是负责学校每年的舞会（Homecoming，Winter Formal，Prom），这其中包括了在学校里制作并张贴大型海报、制定舞会主题及票价和舞会当天的组织安排。Rally（集会）也是他们一手操办，从舞台布置、表演流程到主持人，全是通过 ASB 安排的。ASB 的能人们都会剪辑视频和拍摄，每次集会最有意思的时候就是看他们做的视频。

与其他社团不同的是，因为 ASB 工作量大，所以这是一门单独的课，而不是午餐或课后的活动。

• PAL（Peer Assistance Leadership）：我知道 PAL 的成员每周一都会走到 9 年级教室，为他们介绍学校环境，并且帮助新生适应学校。他们每年还会举办红丝带周（Red Ribbon Week），让学生认识毒品的危害性，以及 Walk in my Shoes Week，通过匿名同学的视角，让他们讲自己的故事，把同学内心不敢说的故事通过匿名者的方式表达出来。在我看来，PAL 更像一个心理医生，疏导同学，万事想开点。

• HRC（Human Relation Council）：目

标是消灭学校里因种族或各种原因受到的不平等待遇。他们每年都会组织相关的特殊活动，叫作 Be kind to your mind campaign。通过每天在学校的日常公告中插入有关精神疾病数据的视频，让同学们对精神疾病及其危害性有更加深入的了解。他们还是 LGBTQ 的支持者，支持性少数群体。我 10 年级的西班牙语老师是这个组织的指导老师，每次都会很激动地和我们阐述他（菲律宾裔）对种族的看法以及他年轻时在学校遭受到的霸凌及不平待遇。每次讲到敏感话题，他就会特别亢奋，顺便宣传 HRC。

• AYS（At Your Service）：学校最年轻领导力社团，创立于 2015 年。致力于为同学寻找更多更好的社区活动和实习岗位。因为美国高中规定学生要做到指定小时的社区服务（Community service hour），所以 AYS 在为学生提供活动机会的同时，更能为学生找到自己喜欢的项目，从而引导同学找到自己今后想参与的工作。在完成社区服务的同时，结交新朋友，更加深入地了解一个社区的运作。

●NHS（National Honor Society）：国家荣誉协会。它是最难进，也是最热门的领导力社团。每年只收 50 个人，但是报名的人数远远超过录取的人数。他们在学校的作用也显而易见：荣誉协会；抵制作弊剽窃；支持诚信。他们每年会有 Integrity Week（诚实周）引导学生不要作弊，而是要做一名廉正的学生。他们还会提供辅导服务，为学习上有困难的同学做免费的辅导老师，鼓励同学们通过自身的努力获得好成绩而不是偷瞄别人的卷子。

每个社团招收的人数不等，PAL 招收的学生非常少，在 30 个左右。其他的社员都控制在 50 个左右，不会超过这个人数。而且年级越高，被录取的可能性就越小。虽然每年的社员都是重新选择的，但是上一年就在社团里的老社员其实是"自动"录取的，这属于不成文的规定。我也观察了每年的社团人选，变动不会很大，固定班底就放在那里。

面试的时候会问什么问题？每个社团的问题都不一样，但都是有大方向的。要提前研究并了解每个社团的目标，才能在面试的时候回答得流利。每个社团都会问的几个问题是（和考大学挺像）：你为什么选我们而不是其他社团？你的到来会给社团哪些好处？（套路）还有更加细节的问题，比如说，AYS就会问：你做过哪些社区活动？在社区活动中你收获了什么？NHS会问：你对诚信的定义是什么？当然，也会有一些无厘头的问题，根本没办法准备。我在 10 年级参加 NHS 面试的时候，被问：你会把你自己形容成什么水果？我根本不知道，草草结束了面试。很多都是需要临场发挥的，不要紧张是非常重要的一点！

领导力社团对于不同学校来说是不一样。我九年级读的学校里，NHS不需要选拔就可以参加，所以就和普通的社团没什么两样。而我现在读的学校非常不同，NHS是学校里最受欢迎的社团之一，挤破头都进不去。而且领导力社团每位同学只能选一个，参加了一个就不能参加另一个。我也不知道大学招生官对于领导力社团的看法是怎么样，到底是重视还是无所谓？不得而知。

我个人和领导力社团的缘分是从10年级转到新学校后开始的。一般领导力社团的选拔都是春季（3、4月），若今年你被录取了，就在秋季新学年开始参与活动。我错过了所有的面试，所以我在10年级的春季报名了NHS。当时我是觉得NHS读着很顺，抱着试试的心态，就报了名。当然结果就是没有结果，因为面试的时候紧张没有发挥好，并且那年NHS的报名人数创历史新高，更是没有录取的可能。AYS的面试时间与其他四个不同，是每年 9 月开始的，我 11 年级抱着试试的心态参加了 AYS 的面试。（然而从今年开始，AYS 的面试日期也改到了春季）我个人喜欢 AYS 的原因是这个社团是做实事的，是一个能够帮助身边人、帮助社区的媒介。不像其他的几个领导力社团，只是每个学期举办一个活动就结束了。AYS 是一个长期的社团，影响力的范围更加广。

我在和一个学姐聊天的时候，她给我讲了一个她朋友的故事。她成绩很好，GPA 超过 4.0，从 10 年级到 12 年级年年申请了 NHS，但是没有一年被录取。这背后的原因是她在学校不够热门（popular），社团的背后也要"靠关系"，你和社团里的某一个人关系好，说不定你就有机会被录取。如果你在学校里没有什么影响力，被录取的可能性就瞬间化为零。

领袖组织的水分多，在报名之前，还是先和同学及学长们聊一聊，不要到最后吃了亏。

Are leadership groups on
campus nominal?

Schools in the U.S. strongly emphasize leadership skills, therefore there are various leadership groups on campus. In DBHS, the only group that required a try-out was Assistant Student Body (ASB). Other than that, all "leadership groups" were led by clubs which did not require any try-out processes.

In CdM, there are 5 leadership groups and they all require application and interview to finalize the members:

● ASB (Assistant Student Body): This is the most fun-loving group among all 5 groups. They organize Homecoming, Winter Formal, and Prom every year. This includes determining themes and ticket prices for every dance, putting up posters around the campus, and organizing the event on that specific day. ASB also takes care of everything and manages the rallies from posters, themes, to training MCs. Another fascinating aspect of this is that ASB makes the best videos because they are professional video editors. The best part of rallies is watching the videos they produced.

Unlike other leadership groups, ASB counts as a class because they have heavy works to accomplish.

● PAL (Peer Assistance Leadership): All PAL members walk into different freshman classes every Monday, introduce the school environment to the newcomers and provide tips for them to adapt high school life. They hold multiple events every year, for example, Red Ribbon Week shows students the danger and consequences of drug usage, and Walk in my Shoes Week enables students to express their current concerns in an anonymous way which is a great approach in empowering students to speak up their minds, stand up for their rights and go above and beyond their potentials. In my opinion, PAL is the "psychologist" on campus to help those who might have potential psychological concerns and risks.

• HRC (Human Relation Council): Eliminating the discrimination on campus is the ultimate goal of HRC. Every year, they have a special campaign to promote equality. Last year, they had a campaign called "Be Kind to your mind". The campaign showed the negative effects of mental illness by providing research data on school broadcast. This year, they created a new campaign named "I am a Human". The leaders advocate unconditional love with no race, gender, or religious boundaries. And they are also active LGBTQ promoters. My Spanish 1 teacher is the instructor of HRC. He talked to us about his childhood story as a Filipino immigrant and the bully he faced in school when he was young. When we discussed controversial topics, he would become extremely sensitive and express his point of view while promoting HRC. He killed two birds with one stone.

• AYS (At Your Service): The youngest leadership program on campus was established in 2015. They promote better community service events and internship programs for students of every interest. Since all American high school students need to have a set amount of community service hours (the number of hours are different from school to school), AYS provides opportunities for students to get the community hours they need while giving them opportunities to find their interest and potential career paths. It is a great opportunity to make friends and learn more about how a community functions.

• NHS (National Honor Society): NHS is the most "prestigious" leadership group on campus. They accept 50 members every year but the number of applicants far exceeds the 50 spots. As the name suggests, they promote integrity on campus and discourage cheating. They have an "Integrity Week" campaign every year to raise the awareness of academic honesty. The members of NHS need to complete 10 hours of community service every month, therefore they are also tutors for those students who have difficulties with certain subjects.

Different leadership groups admit different amount of students every year. PAL only admits around 30 members every year. Other groups admit around 50 members but won't exceed this amount of people. The other trend I noticed is that it is harder to get in as an upper classman. Although every group selects new members every year, the old members are "automatically" admitted even though they need to go through the interview process again.

What did the board members ask during the interview? Every group is slightly different since they have different emphasis for their campaigns. Therefore, understanding every club's specialty is important for the success during the interview. Every leadership group will possibly ask the following questions: "Why do you choose our group instead of other leadership groups on campus?"; "What benefit can you bring to our group?". There are also more detailed questions based on the club, for example, AYS asked me "What community service have you participated in before? What did you learn during your volunteering period?" For NHS, they will definitely ask you your definition of integrity. Sometimes, the questions are unpredictable. When I tried out for NHS during sophomore year, I was asked: What fruit will you describe yourself as? I had no clue on how to answer that question therefore the interview was not the most successful one. A lot of interviews require impromptu conversation, don't panic is important!

I need to clarify that the same leadership group will have different definitions among schools. For example, NHS is a basic leadership club in DBHS with no try-out process. But for CdM, NHS is the most popular leadership group on campus with the coolest kids. Every student can only participate in one of the five leadership groups to provide more opportunities for students to become leaders on campus. I am dubious about the college admissions' perspective in terms of leadership groups, is it crucial? Or it doesn't matter at all?

I started to apply for leadership groups when I transferred to CdM. I waited till the spring of sophomore year to apply because most groups select members for the next school year in spring. I only applied to NHS because I loved the philosophy of the club. Of course, I wasn't admitted because NHS received the greatest number of applications that year and it was extremely competitive.

AYS started their interview process during the beginning of the fall semester unlike the other groups and I participated in the interview for various reasons. (AYS's interview process starts to synchronize with other leadership groups in spring, 2017) First, I love community service and this is the principle of AYS. Second, AYS has influence throughout the community beyond the jurisdiction of the school itself. Third, it is the group that provides students with concrete benefits in the long run. (I noticed that other groups would simply run a campaign) Luckily, I was admitted to AYS.

Seek advice from students with prior experience before try-out to avoid suffering losses.

游学记：印第安纳州，这是个什么（鬼）地方？

2016 年的 7 月，我去了在 Indiana University（印第安纳大学）媒体学院主办的高中生新闻夏令营（High School Journalism Institute）。学校在距离州首府印第安纳波利斯（Indianapolis）一小时车程的布卢明顿（Bloomington），这地方除了有个走不到尽头的大学，其余都是农村，什么都没有。但这里有著名的商学院（Kelley School of Business）以及传媒学院（Indiana University Media School）。

这是一个大学校。打个比方，我们的宿舍在 Spruce Hall，而我们上学的地方在传媒学院 Ernie Pyle，单程就要将近 1 个英里（1.6 公里）。如果倒霉的话，还会遇上美国中部特有的雷阵雨，那就是一个灾难。没有人会开车送你去教室，只能淌着大水，撑着雨伞，用脚走：早上上课要走路，中午吃饭要步行到食堂再回宿舍，下午再重复一次，有时晚上还会有课，还要再走一回。但是这两周我的步行排行榜一直处于朋友圈上游，我就权当减肥。住的宿舍是三年前新造的，有大大的窗户，降暑的中央空调，亮堂干净的淋浴房，晚上不会断的 WiFi。比起老牌的大学，这幢宿舍楼简直是天堂！

言归正传，我读的叫做 HSJI（High School Journalism Institue），是一个在传媒学院举办的新闻夏令营。选课的范围很广，有最基础的新闻写作（News Writing），到摄影写作（Photojournalism），再到视频剪辑（Multimedia）。一个课程为 5 天，每天早上 8:30～11:30 和下午 1:30～4:00 为课堂时间。每节课都有不同的安排，有的课上会有客座讲师或是出外景找素材写文章。

晚上还会有 Break-Out Session，老师把课上的同学分散到不一样的讲座上听课，然后把学到的知识以图文形式做报道上传至网站。

第一周我选择了 Web Packaging，说白了就是将故事、视频、音频和图片打包成为一篇文章。有团队合作为特别讲师写报道的，也有自己找素材自由发挥的。老师希望我们在一周内，每天尝试一种自己以前从来没有使用过的报道方式。我和我的团队为特别讲师 Tom French 做了一个 Adobe 的 Spark Page，将照片与文字放在一起，呈现出一种滚动杂志的效果。有兴趣的朋友可以（翻墙到）谷歌上搜索 HSJI，点开 Student Gallery 看看学生们写的文章。

找素材的时候，还能顺便参观校园。看看人情味十足的钢琴家铜像；给夏天可以当游泳池降温的大喷泉拍张照；还能捕捉到在复古的大楼前的画家；在草丛里找找吃果子的小松鼠，大学里的小松鼠居然不！怕！人！

第二周，我选择了 Multimedia。这是一节学习基本视频剪辑的课程。教我们的老师是 IndyStar 的记者，名叫 Bob Scheer，长得特别像奥巴马。同学们都特别佩服他，因为他在推特（Twitter）上是有认证的大 V。

从课程开始的第一天，老师就让我们拿着手机出门做采访拍视频，问的问题很简单，从"今天的天气怎么样"开始问，可以自己加上跟进问题（Follow up）。我剪辑了一个小视频，看看我和同伴采访到的路人都怎么说。（看视频请翻阅我的公众号历史记录）

第二天便开始和大型摄像机与巨重的三脚架打交道，为第三天的外景做练习。第三天全班同学前往了距离学校三十分钟的一个小镇集市（Lawrence County Fair），两两一组在大太阳下找素材、做采访。我和同伴走过羊圈、牛圈、马圈，一个一个人问过来，看看有没有什么有趣的故事。老师也给予我们很大的帮助，帮助我们找素材，帮我们判断采访有没有价值。最后，我们找到了当天绵羊竞赛的冠军，让她给我们讲了讲她训练羊的故事。

采访（A Roll）好之后，还需要拍很多小花絮（B Roll）来填补采访剪辑跳跃的片段。剪辑的时候还会遇到很多困难，比如说，发现拍出来视频的色度、曝光度不够理想；视频背后有太多杂音；用到最后发现花絮拍的太少了不够用。最后将视频拖来拖去，剪辑了来来回回几十遍，终于做出来一个还算满意的作品。

我和同伴的作品被老师评为 Teacher's Choice，是老师最喜欢的作品。而我和同学们选出来的第一是另一组的视频。他们采访了集市上 4 家卖柠檬茶（Lemonade）的店铺，问 4 名店主同样的问题，比较每家店的不同之处。最后配上欢快的音乐，诙谐幽默引得全班哄堂大笑。

最有趣的是，我们班的同学都很聊得来，天天一起去上课，一起去食堂吃饭，一起待在大堂里聊天。老师也很惊讶我们整个班级这么聊得来。在短短的两周内，我收获了知识、友谊和美食。在印第安纳最开心的还属天天走路，这是我在加州从来不会做的事情。作业多的时候不想去健身房，需要出门就是用车代替双脚。天天在烈日下采访让我身体的毛孔都打开了，出汗洗澡的时候感觉一整天的苦和累都是值得的。

唯一的缺点是这个夏令营的时长太短了，只有两个星期。11年级的暑假我想去一个不一样的学校，读一个时间更长的夏令营，更加深入地了解一个城市，了解每一个同学。

最后说一句：It is an institute, not a camp。是不是这样听上去更有学问？

Summer 2016: Why am
I in Indiana?

In July of 2016, I went to the High School Journalism Institute program in Indiana University, Bloomington. The school was an hour drive away from Indianapolis and there was nothing in town except this enormous college. But Indiana University offers top business programs in Kelley School of Business and the Indiana University Media School is also famous nationwide.

The campus is huge. To give an example, all students live in Spruce Hall and the classrooms are located in Ernie Pyle Hall, the distance between dorm and classroom is nearly 1 mile. If we were not lucky enough, we would face the typical mid-west weather – pouring rain, which is a disaster. No one would accompany you to class, therefore the only option left was holding your umbrella, walking to the class, and enjoying the rainy weather. A lot of my Californian friends would love rainy days because California is dry all the time and rainy weather is new to them. I grew up in Shanghai, China, where it could rain for one month straight in June therefore I don't like rainy weather at all. Walking on campus was extremely painful when you had to get lunch at a different location, walk back to the dorm, and then repeat the whole process again for the afternoon session. During the program, I was usually on the top of the list among all my friends on WECHAT's health report. (The Chinese "facebook" with over 800 million active users every single day) I told myself that all the walk counts as workout, it keeps me fit and skinny. For the two weeks that I spent at IU, I did the most walking in the entire year.

The best part of HSJI was making new friends from another part of the U.S. Going to class and cafeteria together for lunch and dinner, talking in the lounge area at night, and touring the town after class. The institute had a spectacular dorm built 3 years ago. The rooms had enormous windows, cooling air conditioner, unlimited WIFI, and big and clean shower rooms. Compared to many other universities, these dorms were DREAMS!

I attended the program that was part of the media school called "HSJI" which stands for "High School Journalism Institute". There were various courses to choose from, from basic News writing, to Photojournalism, to Multimedia. Each course was 5 days in length, 8:00 – 11:30 AM and 1:30 – 4:00 PM time slots. Every day brought a unique perspective to HSJI because there were special speakers coming in to talk to all the students, or there might be outside field projects.

At nights, there were break-out sessions during which the teacher assigned students to different lectures, asked them to bring back their thoughts through writing coverage on WordPress, and shared it with all students eventually.

For the first week, I chose Web Packaging which was basically putting story, pictures, videos, and sound bites together into a package. The instructor would assign individual projects, or group projects to cover guest speakers. The instructor expected us to utilize different tools every day and create something new that we had never tried before. My favorite post was the coverage for the guest speaker, Tom French. My group and I put together an Adobe Spark Page which was something fun and I had never done before.

When walking around campus, I sought for special ideas to include in my content, I had a chance to explore the campus at the same time. On campus, I encountered the greatest number of squirrels I have ever seen at one location which was completely unlike Los Angeles.

During the second week, I took Multimedia. It was a basic video editing class instructed by Bob

Scheer, a photojournalist from IndyStar. His figure reminded me of Barack Obama a lot. On the first day of class, he impressed every student in the room with his verified twitter account.

Since there was no cushion time for the class, Bob put us into groups and asked us to find random people on campus for interviews regarding the weather on the first day. We could add any follow up questions if we wanted to. After filming their responses, we gathered together to talk about the pros and cons of the videos and the ways in which we could improve next time.

Starting the second day, we used the professional video cameras and giant tripods in order to prepare for the county fair event on the next day. On the third day, we went to the Lawrence County Fair 30 minutes away from school. Working in pairs (I worked with the girl from Beverly Hills High School), we sought for interesting and unique characters in the fair and conducted an impromptu interview based on their personal experiences. Bob helped us to decide the right interviewee with stunning background and a unique story to tell. After walking through llama pen, sheep pen, cow pen, and pig pen, we decided to interview the Sheep's Showmanship Winner, Savannah Speer. She was not like others because she knew how to answer a question and would give a brilliant response. (You can find the video on YouTube: "Savannah's Sheep Show", or subscribe me on WECHAT: BettyTheScientist to find the coverage)

The video contained both A Roll (the actual interview) and B Rolls, which were the little clips inserted in between interview segments. My partner and I struggled when editing the video. We couldn't find the appropriate B rolls to fill the gaps. Sometimes the lighting of clips was awfully dark, or may be there was noise in the background. Sitting in front of the iMac for more than 5 hours, edited back and forth for more than 50 times, we uploaded the video right at 4:00 PM before the deadline. This made my partner and I really appreciate teamwork and achieve a great sense of accomplishment.

At the end, the video made by my partner and I received the Teacher's Choice Award. However, our whole class picked another group's video as Students' Choice Award. They interviewed 4 different lemonade stands at the fair, asked them the same set of questions, compared the differences between each stand. The hilarious response and melodic background music made all students laugh nonstop.

Getting along with all students, learning about journalism from scratch, enjoying Mother Bear's Pizza across the street were only some of the wonderful highlights of my summer. Walking 10 miles a day was not normal for a California girl, but I enjoyed it because it reminded me how much I used to walk from places to places when I was in Shanghai. At the end of a long day, the shower just washed all the exhaustion away and soothed me ready for the next day.

The only weakness of the institute was that it was too short. I didn't have enough time to know everyone better. I highly recommend students to attend a 3 – week or 4 – week program so that they can connect with their instructors and peers on a deeper level.

I have to repeat one more time, "It is an institute, not a camp." (This probably sounds more pedantic?)

留学新生选课记

　　Mall 里挂起了 Back-to-school 的吊牌，无不提醒着我们新的学年即将到来。开学的第一站，便是选课。在学校里帮助选课的老师叫做 GLC（Grade Level Coordinator），或者直接叫 Counselor，也相当于升学顾问，会一直陪伴新生 4 年，直到高中毕业。GLC 说他们就像学生学校里面的爸爸妈妈，他们关心着我们的校园生活，为我们解决难题，充当着中国学校"班主任"的作用。

　　先来给大家普及一下美国高中 4 年每一年级学生的叫法：9 年级的学生叫 freshman，10 年级的学生叫 sophomore，11 年级的学生叫 junior，12 年级的学生叫 senior。同样，大学 4 年每个年级的学生叫法也是这样。

　　GLC 会根据每个人不同的情况来进行选

课。英语和数学是必修课，是高中4年都要上的，但英语和数学也有不同，英语是不能跳级而数学则可以根据程度来安排相应的课程。九年级的美国学生与中国学生不同的是，他们不是一年里面把理化全都上完，而是有选择性的。你可以选择九年级修世界历史，然后十年级修生物，再修化学、物理，一级一级学上去。还有一门课程是九年级学生必修的，别无选择，那就是体育课。但如果在这一年里的加州统一体育考试中取得理想的成绩，在十年级就可以不上体育课了，而是可以上舞蹈课或瑜伽课。其他就有选择范围了，根据自己的喜好选科目，可以是美术，也可以是乐队或第二语言。语言必修两年，若在加州并想进入UC大学，建议连续读一门语言三年。

今年我选择了管乐队、几何课、英语课、世界历史、体育课，还有一门必修的电脑课。因为我吹长笛，所以进了管乐队。如果是学习弦类乐器（大、中、小提琴）则可以进Orchestra（管弦乐队）。中国人最热衷于孩子学的钢琴在美国乐队里最多只有一个人弹，所以学习钢琴在美国高中的乐队并不是很吃香。如果想要孩子能够进入学校的乐队，最好再学一门别的乐器。学校的 Marching Band（军乐队）也是十分出彩。军乐队需要一边走正步一边演奏，因为要参加各种比赛，训练十分辛苦，而且每周有两天放学后要在学校训练到天黑，所以军乐队成员有个特权：不用上体育课!!!

几何课学习的范围广，但内容比较浅显，与中国数学学习的范围小而深不同。而历史课和中国的学习方法又是倒一倒，美国的历史课学的不仅范围广，而且学习的内容也很细致，所以我认为历史考试是较难的。因为历史书上内容很多，又不知道老师会抽什么题目进行检测，第一次考试没有掌握看书的方法导致没有发挥出最好的成绩。到了第二次便吸取经验，将书上的内容过两遍，让大脑有记忆，到了考试的时候便拿了高分。历史考试给我留下了很深刻的印象，虽然我们考试一般都是考选择题，但是不要以为老师批出来的成绩就是最终留在成绩册上的成绩。因为历史考试内容很广，所以大家的成绩一般都比较不好看。老师会给我们机会与他进行辩论，来争取说自己的答案是正确的。如果老师觉得你说的相对合理，他就会把分数给你，这样最后的分数就会好很多。这也告诉我，在美国，什么东西都是要靠自己争取来的，没有谁会把分数白白送给你。

体育课学习的内容很多，我本来以为我的运动细胞还是挺好的，但是到了美国还是吓了一跳。我们开学学习的第一个内容便是游泳，一游便是 5 个星期，天天都游。老美体力太好，我看着他们游泳我都累，我在水里游的时候更是体力透支，累到不行。美国孩子的运动量大我也是见识到了，在中国我最多跑个 800 米，在美国，长跑考试翻个倍，1600 米。还有各种各样别的运动项目，也都是在中国从未尝试过的，对我而言十分具有挑战性。

英语课对我来说反而不是最难的。这里的英语课和中国的完全不一样，我在中国，老师的重点就是教语法，教语法，教语法，一切的一切都是为了中考在做准备。而在美国，我们就是读文章，读文章，读文章，阅读各种各样的故事，有长篇小说，也有短篇小说。老师会针对文章与同学进行讨论与思考，接着再读文章。除了读教科书，我们每个月要读一本课外书，读好书后会考一个关于文章内容的试，来考量对于书籍理解了多少，作为一次小测验的成绩。

还有一门我认为比较难的课程是电脑课。出乎我的意料，电脑课真的不简单。这门课程是加州高中生如果要上大学的话必修的课程，学习的内容是 Microsoft 的各种文档。听起来很简单，但是学起来可没那么容易，这门课程几乎覆盖了 Word、Excel、PPT 文档的全部内容，而且每个章节老师还要进行考试，又是全英语的，除了历史，我学习的时间花的最多的就是电脑课。电脑课上半个学期，还有半个学期学习的是健康课，也是加州学生高中毕业的必修课。

我们的上课时间是 8：00—15：00，老师从来不拖堂，不放学留学生补习（除非是学生自愿补习），也从来不占用课余时间，对于一个以前在中国上学，老师占用放学时间讲题的学生来说，到美国简直像来到了天堂。Freshman（9 年级学生）每天 6 节课，每节课在一个小时左右，除了有个 15 分钟的大休息，以及中午 45 分钟的吃饭时间，其余的课间休息只有 6 分钟，对于偌大的校园，又是走班制的，必须在开学前摸清路线，找到最合适的步行线路，保证开学后每天可以准时抵达教室。Sophomore（10 年级学生）

及以上年级的同学如果参加乐队，那为了不影响正常的学习就必须牺牲睡觉时间，早一个小时(7:00)上学了，每天上 7 节课。

美国孩子的学习生活也不容易啊！

如何培养"女汉子"

体育课是美国进入高中第一年作为一名Freshman的必修课，但有一个群体例外，那就是参加军乐队的成员们。因为每周两次的放学训练，这运动量就已经达标了，边吹奏乐器边走正步可不是闹着玩的，在洛杉矶这种一年四季阳光明媚的地方，在太阳底下晒个一两个小时，可是极大的考验。几乎每个星期五都会有一场橄榄球比赛（因为秋天是橄榄球赛季），不仅是主场要给球队加油鼓劲，客场更是要为球队增强士气。再加上几乎每个星期的周末都要参加各种各样的游行活动，所以周末想睡懒觉是没机会了。周末基本上早晨五六点到学校集合，穿上厚重的军乐队服饰，就浩浩荡荡出发了。如果去迪斯尼进行游行的话，还要再早，凌晨3点学校集合！苦的不仅仅是学生自己，更是学生家长，在洛杉矶这种公共交通不是非常便利的城市，父母还要一大早送小孩，可谓是生理心理的双重考验。军乐队也因此成为了磨炼意志的一个团体。

言归正传，来谈谈体育课。每个学校的设施不一样，所以运动项目也肯定会有所不同。我们学校去年斥巨资造了一个豪华的大泳池，所以在炎热的夏季，开学第一课便是游泳啦。开学第一个星期老师要讲规则、分配更衣箱，所以第一个星期就浪费了。真正的游泳是从第二个星期开始的。一个小时的一节课，减去前后换衣服的时间，真正游泳的时间在 35 分钟左右，但是这 35 分钟的训练量也是蛮猛的。来回不停地游，游泳池的水又很深，脚完全碰不到地面，想偷懒休息一会儿就别想了，光光抓着游泳池边就已经蛮累了。想偷懒不游泳？你想多了，不游泳的话，你就走楼梯吧，接受火辣辣太阳的直射，还有额外的笔头作业要写，还不如清清凉凉地游个泳呢。游泳游5个星期就结束了，本以为可以结束天天带着湿嗒嗒的泳衣的生活了，结果被告知明年5月份再游一个月。5月份的洛杉矶还是很冷的呢！跳入冰冷的泳池还是需要勇气的。最痛苦的还是姑娘们，头发长还没有时间吹干头发，铃响后便奔向冰冷的空调教室，必须带好外套预防感冒。

接下来的一个单元是体育模拟测试，为明年3月份的加州统一健康测试做准备。考试项目十分全面，为了考量学生的综合水准，花了将近5个星期才陆陆续续完成测试。考验耐力的测试有两个，1英里长跑（正正好好等于我在中国跑两个800米），然后是一个20米的来回跑（Pacer），跟着录音的节奏越跑越快，越到后面越难跑。考验手臂力量的则有俯卧撑和改良版的引体向上（相对来说更加简单，就是躺在地上，手抓着一个杠子，然后用手臂力量将身体向上拉，要下巴碰到一个衡量物才算通过）。还有一个需要吊在一个很高的杠子上，下巴要停留在杠子上方，能挂多久就算多久。还有改良版较容易的仰卧起坐和正常的坐位体前屈。量身高体重肯定是测试的一部分，老师还有一个很秘密武器，把体重身高输进去然后握着那个仪器便可以测量一系列身体的数据，综合评估后得出肥胖指数（BMI）。

这一系列测试对于一个中国孩子来说还是很具有挑战性的，因为很多都是以前没有尝试过的，幸好我的运动细胞还算不错，在上海学校里是可以在年级跑步拿名次的，所以这些体育项目对我来说还不是特别的难。唯一一项我害怕的是1英里长跑，因为这是以前训练的整整两倍！虽然说我喜欢跑步，但这运动量来的实在有点突然，接受不了。但人性化的是，老师会提前告诉我们哪天要长跑，可以提前准备运动饮料，然后跑步的时候老师允许同学戴耳机听音乐来放松，有助于加快跑步速度。在跑步的过程中也是允许走路的，只要你能在规定时间内完成规定任务。通过 3 月份的考试非常重要，因为这样才能保证你在十年级可以选择你喜欢的体育项目进行发展。女孩子通常喜欢选择跳舞，因为一直是呆在室内的，可以吹空调又不用晒太阳。男孩子则比较喜欢练肌肉，可以专门选择练肌肉的科目。如果通不过考试呢？十年级再选一次体育课，但这次又通不过呢？也没办法了，美国高中就上两年的体育课。所以你想十年级多修一门主课，把体育课留到 11 年级或 12 年级再上也是可以的。

最奇葩的还属高尔夫单元，去哪里打球呢？组团去球场？不可能，我们学校的运动场这么大，肯定得好好利用！充分利用资源，用棒球场来代替高尔夫球场。结束高尔夫单元后是练习跳舞。第一学期的体育课就这么结束了。下半学期的内容基本上就是把这个学期的体育课内容倒一倒。除了上体育课，每个星期还有一天是在教室里学习体育知识的，还会有考试。体育课可不是这么好上的啊！

学校除了军乐队，还有一个特殊的团体，他们也不用上体育课，但他们做的事还是和体育课性质很接近的，那就是运动队。美国人的运动细胞众所周知，他们的运动队也是各种各样，丰富多彩。男/女高尔夫、篮球、网球、足球、橄榄球、棒球、田径、长跑、羽毛球、排球、游泳队……每项运动在赛季开始前会进行选拔活动，运动队都会在学校里"贴小广告"来吸引人才加入。参加了运动队，你就可以不上体育课了，改成每天的最后一节课训练。

美国高中的运动课程丰富多彩，经过小学、初中的磨炼，美国学生身体的耐力、灵敏度也是出乎我的意料，那些看似娇小的女孩子其实运动起来也是一个个女汉子。听说我们学区里的一个初中，有个老师要求他的学生每天跑 1 英里，我想耐力就是这样培养出来的吧。总之，来美国，做好体育课体力透支的准备，往好的地方想，就当减肥。

不给糖就捣乱？

Halloween 的拼写是怎么来的呢？All hollows' evening 是万圣节最初的名字，意为"天下圣徒之日"，这一天是古代凯尔特民族（Celtic）的新年，为了避免幽灵的干扰，孩子们会挨家挨户讨糖果，进行"Trick or treat"（不给糖就捣乱）的活动来赶走幽灵，这个活动已经进行了三千年了！后来，人们就将 All hollows' evening 简称为 Halloween。

在 Halloween 的前一周，校园的墙上就会贴满海报，图书馆里也用各种骷髅和巫婆进行装饰，这无不提醒着 Halloween 的来临。每年的 Halloween，学校里面也会举行各种各样的活动进行庆祝。比如说，我们学校就有组织免费的万圣节电影之夜，每年也会评选"年度最佳装扮"（最可爱、最疯狂、最搞笑……），每个社团也会举行不同的庆祝活动，会利用午餐时间举办 party。

在万圣节当天，我们学校是允许穿自己的戏服去上学，我们学校相对而言比较自由，可不是每个学校都允许同学穿自己奇奇怪怪的衣服去上学的！但是，这也不意味着你想穿什么就穿什么，学校里还是会广播 dress code（着装标准）：不能化太恐怖的妆容，着装也不能与烟草/酒饮/毒品相关。总的来说，学校还是欢迎你穿积极向上的戏服来上学的。万圣节当天一走进校门就像走进了迪斯尼乐园一般，有很多人装扮成电影里的卡通人物。我还看到很多男生穿成士兵的样子，或者打扮成自己喜欢的名人。学校里令我印象最深刻的一套服装是我体育课的一个男生，为了扮成"二战"时期德国的电报员，他头戴 5 磅的头盔，身上背着个假的电话，穿着一身迷彩服，也真是活灵活现。他的这身打扮也引起了众多同学的围观，我没挤进去，没拍到照片，有点可惜。我则打扮成了史迪奇（Stitch）的样子，我的一个朋友打扮成了Lilo。（Lilo&Stitch是一部出名的迪斯尼电影！）今年其实在校园里有很多人和我"撞衫"，其中就包括我的一个朋友，但撞衫没关系，万圣节开心最重要！

同学来学校的时候，一般都会随身带着糖果，分给朋友们，一起分享快乐。而在这一天，虽然说不放假，但是老师一般都会做一些有趣的活动，或者把上课的时间缩短一点，留给同学聊天的时间。比如说历史课上老师就给我们看了一个关于万圣节来历的视频，不但有趣，同时也和他教的科目有着千丝万缕的关联。体育课也有一个特例，因为同学穿着较为复杂，为了不浪费时间，老师允许你穿着自己的衣服上体育课，准备活动也可以免了！同时，在这一天老师也会分享糖果给同学们吃。今天给我印象最深刻的是上英语课的时候，我们老师不仅给了我们糖果，还给了我们她前一天亲手制作的布朗尼纸杯蛋糕！上面用骷髅糖果进行点缀。虽然很甜，但还是感受得到老师满满的爱。

放学后，一般同学都会和好朋友一起化妆，进行 trick or treating（不给糖，就捣乱），捣腾一下午，在晚上 6:30 左右，出发！

托同学的福，到了学校附近的豪宅小区讨糖，因为这种小区氛围比较好，会有比较多的人家发糖果。有利也有弊，因为小区实在是太大而且小区根本就没有路灯，所以，一定要有大人开车跟在身边，并且在走路的时候打开手电筒，跟着大部队一起走在街边的人行道上，避免发生事故。若看到前面房子没造好或者房子灯没有亮的，立刻上车前往下一条路。晚上乌漆抹黑，还是有点阴森森。

一般来说，如果一家人家门口的灯亮着，就代表他们欢迎你们来拿糖果，如果进门处的灯是暗的，基本上就不用按门铃，走到下一家去，因为这种情况大多数就代表他们不欢迎你们。无论是华人还是外国人，他们都会给你们糖果，就算没有放在门口，他们也会在家里翻出糖果来给你们。那天给我留下最深刻印象的有三家人家。第一家，那对夫妻装扮成了飞行员的样子，十分的酷，这对外国夫妇人也很好，拿出糖果让我们自己抓。第二家，虽然这家人家门前灯是暗的，但别的房间灯是亮的，所以我们还是按了门铃。突然，门旁边的玻璃窗闪出了蓝光，而且蓝光在动！一下子，门就开了，原来是女主人等候在门旁多时，看到有人来便打开了手电筒，吓了我们一跳。最后一家令我印象深刻的是一幢大豪宅的女主人，她们家的花园实在是装饰得太漂亮了！女主人甚至打扮了她们家的狗狗，给她的拉布拉多犬戴上了万圣节标志性的橙色披风。

根据每户人家对万圣节的热情程度不同，给的糖果也很不一样。关于这个，我也选出了我心里的前三名。No.1：应该是一个华人家庭。在给糖果的同时，还送了我们一人一支圆珠笔，而且笔上的装饰品也和糖果相关，十分的应景。No.2：主人很热心地准备了甜甜圈，问我们要吃甜甜圈还是要拿糖果，我拿了甜甜圈，好吃！No.3：我们开门说"Trick or treat"的时候，那位女主人突然问了一句"Candy or bubble"（要糖果还是泡泡糖）。她和我们说她每次都要这么问的理由是有的孩子有可能不喜欢糖果，所以她还会备着泡泡糖，以防不时之需。

万圣节是个不分年龄的节日，想做个孩子的话，换上戏服去捣乱吧。

解读成绩，占比怎么算？

你的成绩怎么来的？大考决定命运？错，完全错了，在美国，老师注重的是平日积累，这是重中之重。

学年的第一堂课便是老师来讲解课堂的行为规范和这学年的学习计划。老师会发一张 syllabus（课程提纲），上面会详细列出课程安排，并且还会罗列出各类作业和测验考试在总成绩中占据的百分比。带回家后还需家长过目并签名。老师还会让家长留下电话号码以及邮箱地址，以便同学若有不做作业或者在课上捣乱之类的不良行为，可以联系家长进行沟通。一般来说，情况不是很严重的时候，老师会发邮件给家长；如果行为十分恶劣，则是直接打电话找上门来。给老师留下基本信息，是对老师工作的支持与帮助。

签 syllabus，便是这个学年的第一项作业。这将是家长们一学年中的第一次签名，但同时也是最后一次签名。我在上海读中学的时候，大考小考天天有，老师要求家长签名签名再签名。不仅家长心烦意乱，同时一种不好的现象也在蔓延——同学的仿签。运气好的同学没被抓到把柄，运气背一点的话，老师联系家长，回家又是一顿"竹笋烤肉"。而在美国，需要签名的作业几乎没有。

　　那么，家长如何了解孩子在学校的学习情况及表现呢？美国从小学开始就有 Parent Portal，其实中文翻译过来，就是一个网上在线查阅成绩的地方。开学前注册好就可以登记一个用户名和密码，然后学校会把每个学生的信息资料打到电脑里，这个查成绩方法对于我爸妈这种"远程操控"来说绝对是一个福音。他们可以在中国随时跟进我的近况。老师一般会把 Assignment（作业）的具体信息发布在网上，也就是我们所说的 Gradebook

Detail（成长手册详细信息）。每一项作业的分值也有所不同，最令我惊讶的是，很多时候考试的分值竟然没有一个 Homework Packet（作业包）的分值高！这也从侧面说明了平时作业的重要性。

Homework packet 是什么？直译过来其实就是一沓作业组成的作业包。美国老师的收作业方式与中国老师有所不同。在上海上中学的时候，班级后面有两个小桌子，需要交的作业一字排开，然后课代表把作业一早统计好交给老师，以便老师尽快批阅并在上课的时候总结讨论作业的问题。美国学校是走班制的，这种收交作业的模式会变得很困难，老师批好后要第二天才能把作业还给你，也就不"新鲜"了。美国老师采取了一种新的收交作业模式，在作业上敲章，证明你完成了功课，而批改作业这件事，就是交给学生自己完成了。这也从另一个角度考验学生的自觉性，只有你自己才能帮自己。老师会在课上报作业答案，同学自己批。因为美国老师教的学生实在是太多了，最少的也有90～100个学生，我的数学老师一天下来有将近200个学生，就算有助教，这也是巨大的工作量。所以，一般作业都是老师评讲，同学提出疑问，老师解答，然后再把作业收上去。我的历史老师做法有略微不同，他还要"懒"。一个章节收一个作业包，这不仅考验学生做作业的积极性，还考验学生的管理能力，是否能保管好作业。有时候，这一沓作业比这个章节的考试分值还来得高！

　　学校每6个星期会往家里发一个成绩单，为了保护隐私，成绩单是密封的，除了你自己，没有人可以从信的外面看到成绩。每所学校有细微不同，但相同的是差不多在学期的一半或者是三分之一的时候，发一张成绩单，以便不看 Parent Portal 的家长了解孩子的学习近况。Freshman（9年级）的影响不是最大但也不能掉以轻心，但 sophomore 和

junior（10、11 年级）的成绩单是大学申请时重要的衡量标准之一，成绩单要好好保管。每 6 个星期发一次成绩单，也可以让学生清楚自己所处的位置。我们老师说，两个 6 weeks grading period 之后（也就是发了两次成绩单之后），成绩的浮动也就不是很大了，因为前面有 12 个星期打下基础，成绩只要没有特别大的失误，是不可能在最后 6 个星期里突然急速下降或升高。所以如果开学 12 周后，成绩在 B，升到 A－的可能性几乎没有，在 B＋的话，还是有可能拿 A－的。还有，求老师也是没有用的，老师根本不吃这一套，他们在成绩面前都是铁面无私的。所以，我建议如果老师若给 Extra Credit（额外加分）的机会，一定要去做，相信我，对成绩的帮助可不是一点点！而且有额外加分的机会特别少，如果有，一定一定要把握！在这里我也告诉大家另外一个事实，开学初期一定要保证成绩是高分，因为学期刚刚开始拿低分，对总成绩的影响是很大的，会把分数拉得很低，很难看，越到后面爬上来越难。但如果拿了低分，也不要怕，认认真真完成老师布置的作业，踏踏实实地复习考试，成绩会慢慢好转的。

　　坚持与积累，掌握了这两点，成绩这个问题就根本不用担心了，放肆地玩耍吧。

三种舞会，三种玩法

　　美国高中生的舞会到底是怎么回事？因为在中国我读的公立学校从来没有这些活动，因此对于舞会更加感到好奇，想要一探究竟。在中国，有些老师甚至会觉得男生女生一起跳舞是很不恰当的行为，而在美国，从中学开始就有许多舞会活动。与中国恰恰相反，在美国，千万别小看舞会这件事！

　　一整个学年一共有三场大型的舞会，分别是 Homecoming（校友日）、Winter Formal（冬季正式舞会）以及 Prom（正式舞会）。每一场舞会都有许多的共同点——都要求着装正式，女生必须穿礼服，而男生也是西装笔挺，都必须要经过精心打扮才能入场。所以，准备来美国读书的同学们，请一定要准备好一套正装哦（当然，你也可以在美国买）！舞会在周末举行，这些活动都需要跳舞，但一般大家都是瞎跳，不必担心舞姿不够优雅。

Homecoming 的举办时间通常是在开学的一个月以后，这个舞会从字面上的意思说起来，其实就是欢迎同学们度过暑假后，重返校园。Homecoming 的正式程度因学校而异（Prom 规格最高，最正式），门票价格也会有所不同。每年都有不一样的 Homecoming 主题，十分引人注目。开学的时候，学校就会贴出预售门票的海报，提前买的话，会有折扣。可是对于一个高中生来说，如果没有家长的赞助，还是很大的一笔费用（而且一买就是两张）。Homecoming 是由男生来邀请女生作为舞伴共同前往（一般都在校外举办），这邀请可不是随随便便地问一下女生她们就会答应的，邀请女生去 Homecoming 也是一门学问！

在 9 月初，刚开学的时候，学校便会花香四溢，很多女生手里都会拿着花。花是哪里来的呢？是男孩子为了邀请她们共同出席Homecoming 舞会送的！同时男生还会大花心思来构造 poster（海报），写下想对女孩子说的话。男孩子们都各出奇招（通常要想办法把女孩子的名字融入到标语中）讨女生欢心。Homecoming 的重头戏还属选出国王与王后。参加的同学都有权利投票并且选出他们最喜爱的男生与女生，通过谈吐、颜值、气质等各方面综合考量后，选出一男一女作为 Homecoming King & Queen。为了争得这个名号，同学们便会格外地卖力。Homecoming 也可以和你的同性朋友一起去哦，就算没人邀请你，你完全可以和朋友去玩玩，作为课余的放松。

Winter Formal，也被称作"优先舞会"，通俗地来讲就是女生选择男生作为男伴出席。和 Homecoming 一样，女生也会做海报邀请男生，并请朋友帮她举海报，协助邀请。女生也会准备礼物给男生以表感谢。最尴尬的时候还属男生不一定会接受女生的邀请！

我在学校听到了一个很有趣的故事。历史课我同学在一天上课的时候，发现桌子上放着一盒未拆封的巧克力，在装巧克力的篮子里还放着一个棒球。我同学也一纳闷，想不通，谁会无缘无故送她巧克力啊！作为一名乖孩子，她把巧克力上交给了老师。老师笑了笑，把巧克力拿了过去。老师对我的朋友说，这是他上节课的一个女孩子邀请同班的男孩子出席 Winter Formal 送的礼物，因为那个男孩子喜欢打棒球，所以那个女孩子还特地在篮子里放了一个棒球。可是那个男生拒绝了女生的邀请。那个女生既生气又尴尬，有可能是一怒之下忘了巧克力这回事儿，下课之后就直接离开教室了。至于那个男孩拒绝的理由，老师也不是特别清楚，有可能是这个男生已经答应了别人的邀请，或者就是纯粹的不想去。

这个故事从侧面告诉我们另一个道理，

去参加舞会这件事，必须要找比较熟悉的朋友一起参加。要不然人家不愿意和你一起去，辛辛苦苦的准备都落空又让自己的处境很尴尬。

上半学年有两场舞会，而下半学年就只有 Prom 一场舞会了。Prom 也被称作毕业舞会。只有学校的高年级——11、12 年级的学生可以参加，Prom 和 Winter Formal 的形式十分相似，也是在校外举行的，是三次舞会中最为隆重的，所有女生都必须穿及踝礼服。男生邀请女生共同参加，在学校的最后两年留下最美好最难忘的回忆。届时也会选出一年一度的 King & Queen。每次舞会都有专业摄影师来给参加的学生拍照片，到时候可以到学校的一个地方领取，留作纪念。

从美国的舞会便能看出，美国人的礼仪培训都是从娃娃抓起的。当中国孩子周末在题海中奋战，猛刷数学题为了在考试中取得好成绩，进入理想学校的时候，美国孩子已经画上眼线，刷好睫毛膏，打扮得漂漂亮亮去参加舞会了。美国人不是死读书，在学校里混得好，更要多参加活动，这样才能认识更多的朋友（因为美国是走班的，每节课的同学都不一样）。这也是很重要的社交方式，还需多多学习。

学生签证惹大祸

　　拿着 I - 20 出国？务必先让学区/学校的招生官在 I - 20 第三页下方的格子里签上名！公立私立都一样！

　　第一学期的期末考试结束后，学校里回响起欢乐的圣诞歌曲，我整理好书包蹦跶蹦跶地走出校园，享受着慵懒的阳光以及不知不觉到来的第一个没有寒假作业的寒假。美国的寒假是在圣诞节的前一个星期开始的，一直放到新年后结束，俗称 Winter Break。带着喜悦的心情，与爸爸妈妈来到阳光灿烂、气候湿润温暖的佛罗里达，行囊里备着夏天的花衣裳，迎合度假的美丽心情。不知不觉，出租车停靠在迈阿密码头。一路安检，排队等待办理上船手续。延绵的队伍丝毫没有影响我的好心情，可谁知，烦心事接踵而至。

与爸爸妈妈一起办理邮轮入住的时候，工作人员帮爸爸妈妈顺利地办好了入住手续，可是在办理我的手续的时候，工作人员首先查看了我的 I－20（证明在美国读书的证件），和他的上司说了点什么，又在电脑上飞速敲打键盘。我以为只是走程序，因为我和爸爸妈妈 B－1/B－2 的身份不一样，我手持的是 F－1 学生签证，有可能操作起来比较复杂，我也就没太在意。终于，那位先生将房卡交入我们手中，我以为我们就可以这样登船了，没想到那位轮船公司的经理找到了我，他说要带我去一个柜台，有人要询问我几个问题，只要如实回答就不会影响上船出海的。我便老老实实跟着去了，没想到，麻烦就这样来了。

　　接待我们的是一位矮矮胖胖的黑人女子，扎着黑人中十分普遍的编发。她接过我的 I－20 证件，粗略查看了一下，便指出了问题。她问我在 I－20 的第三页下方为何没有学区负责人同意出境的签名（因为上船之后便是一条龙服务，所以上船前就会将进关全部办好）？我和妈妈一下子愣了。其实在放假前，妈妈好几个朋友的孩子都在美国的私立学校读书，然后她们都和妈妈说她们孩子的学校在放假前一个月统一发 e-mail 给国际生的家长，让孩子把 I－20 带到学校签名，使他们可以顺利回中国并再次入境美国。当时妈妈想，持 B-1/B-2 签证的人去加勒比不用签证，她便觉得我也是没问题的，也没多想。这样子被人家一问，我们也是傻眼了。后来据我们分析，这些人是要我们证明身份，因为她们要核实我们是不是真的在美国读书。

接下来，我和爸爸妈妈便开始各种想办法。突然想起前段时间我把我学校学区负责人的名片当作书签夹在书里，我便立即拿出来打电话到学区，那时候是 12 月底，所有工作人员都在休假，只有前台一个人，也找不到那名负责人。住在洛杉矶的姑姑立即前往学区，帮我想办法联系负责人。可是前台的人说负责人出国度假了，她们也无能为力。姑姑拜托她们代签，那些学区的人怕担责任丢了饭碗，不肯代签，这条路也是走不通了。接着，我又发邮件告诉招生官我的情况十分紧急，请他快点帮我签名，用邮件或者传真的方式发到轮船公司。这是招生官的工作邮箱，度假时当然不会看，也是碰壁了。看着指针一分一秒接近船离开码头的时间，我绝望地坐在椅子上，仰望着天花板，眺望空无一人的登船大厅。

I-20上没签名的学生被叫到柜台的人不止我一个，其中有许多中国的小留学生，看着他们一个一个解决了签名问题后离开，而我却依然坐在椅子上一动不动。另一个与我命运相同，也找不到负责任人签名的女孩与我坐在一起，而她的情况又和我略有不同。她8年级的时候来美国（现在9年级），那时候第三张上面是有签名的，但是这签名有效期为一年，一年时间已过，签名也无效了，需要学校再新签一次。这女孩子曾经要求学校帮她再签一次，学校硬是不肯，也是无路可走。此时她也没办法联系到负责人。同病相怜的两个女孩，最终还是没成功拿到学区的签名，抱着满满的遗憾，与爸爸妈妈离开了码头，来到机场，愤怒之下，改签了机票当天回到洛杉矶。

可是遇到这种问题的人不仅仅在船码头，更在美国机场。我在学校仅有的几个中国同学中的一个在寒假回国后再回到美国时，也遇到了难题。Selina 住在北京，放假一开始便回国了，由于机票昂贵而且座位很少，所以她在开学后一个星期才回来。她的机票是从北京首都机场飞到旧金山，然后再换乘内陆飞机回洛杉矶。可是在进关的时候，被海关狠狠地拦下了，被领进了被中国人俗称"小黑屋"的询问室。据 Selina 的回忆，她也不知道她说错了什么，便被海关给拦了下来。后来，海关问她为什么在 I－20 第三张没有签字，她也愣了一下，因为她是周日回来的，学区里也没有人帮她证明她的身份。Selina 还错过了回洛杉矶的飞机，海关帮她改签了机票，她人便滞留在了旧金山机场。Selina 在小黑屋里关了三个小时，终于被放出来。她说，海关给了她一个月临时的居留签证，要通过学区负责人在 I－20 签名，然后开一份证明，最后将护照与文件一起寄到华盛顿，才能顺利读完这个学期。

这两个活生生的例子也给我上了一堂课，这是自以为是而犯的错。吸取教训，以后所有事情都要听取多方意见，多上网研究研究，以保证万无一失。

阅读阅读再阅读

在开学之前，我一直有个疑问，美国这英语到底是怎么个学法，难道和中国一样，背背古文，做做阅读？

但是在开学前领书的时候，我就被吓了一跳。推开门进入领书的教室，满屋子的书堆在我的面前，一股书卷气扑面而来。高高低低，书堆得一层又一层。别看领书室书多，但是每个科目及年级的书都排列整齐，分类明确，绝对不会拿错书（不会有奥斯卡拿错信封那样的尴尬事）。进了领书室，便会有专门的工作人员拿着你的课程表（Schedule）核对并且选出你需要的书交给你，最后会将书的条形码扫入电脑，书就是你的啦！整个过程很快，和图书馆借书差不多。唯一的不同，就是学校对教科书极为保护，借书前要先签保证书，内容就是说，如果书被弄坏了，要承担责任进行相应的赔偿。正是有着这个"威胁"，美国学校的图书才能够循环利用，教科书用十几年还是完好无损。

当我拿到数学和历史书的时候，我也没有很惊讶，毕竟一本书读一年，这点厚度是要的。拿到英语书的时候，愣是吓了一跳，这么厚！这一学年读不读的掉？

先来给大家普及一下，新来到美国的学生先要去做一个评估测试，测试英语水平。通过你的听说读写成绩来决定你是读 ELD Program（English language developement，英语需要提高的学生，通常不是美国本土人），Sheltered English（掩蔽教学，就是在与美国孩子上同样课程的同时，进度稍慢，但是期末考试的内容是完全相同的），Regular（正常的英语课）。如果你在初中的 GPA 很高（通常都是满分 4.0），升高中的时候，有一个类别的课程叫作 Honor Class（也就是所谓的荣誉班，上的课程与普通版不同，难度较大，学生的压力也随之增加）。我去年参加入学考的时候，考进了 Sheltered 班，一开始有点遗憾，但后来一想，与正常英语课上的内容是一样的，掩蔽教学的进度相对较慢，也许可以帮助我更好地适应美国的英语环境。

开学前和开学后，我问了很多在美国读书的朋友和认识的新同学，这美国的英语到底是怎么上的？他们都回答不出来，不知道怎么向我解释美国的英语课程。既然他们解释不清，我就只能自己体验了。第一个学期难度并不是很大，开学后老师首先开始了短篇故事单元（fiction），其中的几个故事我并不陌生，莫泊桑的《项链》，欧·亨利的《麦琪的礼物》，还有一些美国作家的科幻故事。内容都能读明白，但是我最大的问题还是词汇量不够。文章里有很多的形容词、动词都是我没看到过的，查生词便成了每天回家后的必修课。每篇文章读下来，生词都在 100

个以上，而且上课老师只是通读全文，在某些重要地方会停下来给我们讲解一下。所以在单词这方面还是要自己抓抓紧，才能够更好地理解文章内容。

第二个单元：学习人物传记，是非小说类的文学作品（nonfiction）。文章相对较短，而且和真实生活比较贴切。相对来说，这类的励志故事比较容易理解。

第三个单元：也是第一个学期的最后一个单元，我们读了荷马的史诗 *The Odyssey*（《奥德赛》），讲述了奥德赛国王在攻打特洛伊战争胜利后，遭受宙斯等希腊神灵的谴责，在奥德赛的回家路上不断地折磨他，经过了 10 年的漫长旅程，才终于回到家乡。由于时间有限，Sheltered 班和正常班的同学读的是书本上的奥德赛，是整本书删减后的 1/3，而荣誉班的同学则要将整本书读完，可见压力有多大。词汇是学习英语文学的难点！这本书里面有很多描述船的部件的词语我一个都不知道，还有各种神灵的名字，也是把我给绕晕了。靠着老师传授的学习方法，我每读完一个故事，便按照段落进行概括，这样在期末考试前的复习也可以比较有针对性。我将生词一一查出，发现只有这样才能够更好的理解文本。刚开始，我让妈妈帮我买了中文版的《奥德赛》帮助阅读，结果发现这书上的内容都是跳着来的，根本找不到在教科书中的哪一章，最后也是放弃了。一定要记住，在学习中遇到问题或者不能理解的难点，请一定要问老师！老师不怕回答你的问题，就是怕不问问题。

本来以为，美国的英语课会像中国语文课那样，每周都有小测验以及考试，结果与我的预想完全相反，除了每个星期的 SAT 单词的考试（每个星期老师会给你 15 个单词，在第二周的周四或周五会进行拼写以及语法的测试），平时几乎连作业也没有，考试更是少之又少。短篇小说单元的考试，是用演讲的形式代替的。老师要求每两个同学为一组，抽签选出一篇读过的文章，进行深层次的解读，并以PPT的形式呈现出来。最后根据制作内容、幻灯片格式和演讲的感染力等因素进行综合评分。第二个单元的考试，由于是人物传记单元，老师就索性让我们写一篇我们自己的故事作为单元评估。因为前大半个学期都是在这种轻松的学习方式中度过的，到了读完《奥德赛》进行期末考试的时候，我完全傻了眼。到现在我还记得我们的考试共有151道题目，从历史背景、文章内容、词语解析和人物性格等各种角度入手，考得我头晕脑胀，完全没有方向。令我记忆犹新的是，让你把故事中的人名和他们所居住的岛屿进行连线，这么多古希腊的岛屿到最后靠着猜和排除法，勉勉强强地完成了试卷。考了个80分居然还是全班的最高分，可见这复习还是有遗漏的地方，而美国老师偏偏考这些偏门的！

额外的，每六个星期老师会带我们去图书馆的电脑上进行一次阅读考试，所以，我们每六个星期便要读一本书，最后这成绩会算进你的英语总分。

美国的英语学起来没有想象中的那么简单，下半学期有诗歌单元，莎士比亚的《罗密欧与朱丽叶》，由讲述美国 20 世纪 30 年代的美国经济大萧条时期加州经济状况的《人鼠之间》（*Of mice and men*）来结束这个学年。我认为 John Steinbeck 的这本书是一部人人必读的经典之作，能让学生更好地了解美国，以及那些光鲜亮丽背后的真实生活。

让我将美国的英语课总结成一句话——阅读，阅读，再阅读。

我的开放日和你的不一样！

美国人的家长会怎么开？坐在教室里面领学生手册，听老师报期末考试名次，布置寒暑假作业？大错特错，美国开家长会也是"走班制"。

在每个学年开学的一个月（9月中）左右，学校会安排某一天的晚上作为"返校夜"（Back to school night）。返校夜的目的就是为了让家长能够更加清楚地了解孩子在学校学的课程，看一下老师是什么样的人（因为美国高中基本上每年的老师都不一样），并且向老师提出对于课程的疑问。整个家长会持续约两个小时，这两个小时平均分配给各科老师，约为 20 分钟。在这 20 分钟里，老师一般只谈总体情况，让家长有个基础的概念，不像中国的家长会喜欢对优秀学生进行表彰。

143

美国老师对孩子更多的是保护，不会透露信息给其他家长形成攀比心理。所以就算是老师要将批好的试卷发还给学生，为了保护个人隐私，老师只会告诉大家班级里的最高分，具体人名是不会透露的。

在返校夜，与学生一样，让家长们在校园里临时充当了一回学生。6分钟的课间休息，从学校的一头跑到另一头，在偌大的校园里寻找下一个教室，对于家长来说也是一次不同寻常的体验。在介绍完大致情况之后，家长可以找老师单独谈话，了解孩子的学习情况。但是，也不要指望老师会记住你孩子的名字，因为他们教的孩子实在是太多了！以我的数学老师为例，她一天教6节课（一节课的休息也没有），每节课40个人，一共240名学生！也不能指望数学老师记住这么多人的名字啊！总的来说，返校夜就是了解孩子在学校的大致情况，而且开学才一个月，所以孩子们的特点也没有完全显露出来，老师也不能太早下定论。

如果家长想对学校有更好的了解，想要知道孩子到底在学点什么，课堂表现到底好不好，第二个学期还有机会！大部分学校在3月中下旬会有一次"开放日"（Open house）。开放日与返校日又有所不同。返校日是家长直接找到孩子的任课老师谈话，而开放日则以学科为单位，向家长们展示学校的面目。届时，每个学科也会进行丰富多彩的以学科内容而展开的活动来吸引家长们的注意。

开放日不仅是家长们的学校参观，更是同学们的积极参与。为了鼓动同学们踊跃参与各项开放日活动，老师便会使出杀手锏——额外加分（Extra Credit）。对于所有的美国学生来说，这机会是弥足珍贵的。因为在正常情况下，老师是不会无缘无故给你加分的，所以我们只能靠好好学习期末拿全 A。但有了额外加分就不一样了，比如说我们健康课（Health，是一门加州高中的必修课）的老师抛出了橄榄枝，在开放日那天晚上，协助前来的家长做健康课的活动（帮助父母量血压，测体重、身高），就能获得额外的 20 分。看起来微不足道，但是这 20 分一加到你总分里可以把总分直接提升 5%！5% 的概念就是，能将一个成绩在 B 的学生拉回 A。如果是光凭好好考试，做作业的话，是不可能在这么短的时间达到的。同样的，我们的数学老师也采取了相同的方法，给附加分，鼓励学生参加数学组推出的 Math Matrix（数学竞赛）。不能参加开放日的同学，可以选择合作做海报，宣传这个活动；或者是到比赛现场给竞赛同学加油鼓气。说到底，老师是鼓励全体同学参与到校园的大型活动中来。

这是我在美国参加的第一次校园日，所以印象还是比较深刻的。最看重这个活动的两个教研组是外语和数学。外语里面就分了许多学科：中文、韩文、西班牙语和法语。因为不是所有人都精通这些语言，所以外语组举行的活动就是唱歌。在中文课上的人唱中文歌，在法语课上的人唱法语歌，各有各的特色。根据每个老师的不同要求，每个班要穿统一色系的衣服，然后根据歌的内容进行夸张的"表演"，给家长与同学们呈现出歌舞剧的效果。在我看来，最有趣的外语班一定是中文 1（Chinese1，是给那些没有中文基础的 ABC或者外国人的中文班）。中文老师让他们唱的歌，歌名就很有趣《对不起，我的中文不好》，是三个美国孩子唱的。为了集体荣誉感与额外加分的诱惑，大家都是硬着头皮上了。

历史课与数学课的开放日活动有些相似——知识竞赛。但这些内容都是在课堂上学过的，完全不会超出提纲。和我以前在电视里看到的比赛有点类似，是抢答形式的。题目出来之后，看谁的"手快"先抢到答题资格。但是，这些游戏还是不太规范（业余水平），有些班级不管三七二十一先抢到了再说，因为答错了也不会扣分。

开放日不仅是了解学校课程，参加各项活动，也是家长找老师聊天的机会。但这是自愿的。开放日，所有的老师全都留在学校，老师都很和蔼，有问必答。特别是到了3月底的选课关头，找老师聊一聊，进行下一学年的课程安排，也能帮助学生与家长减轻一些烦恼。

说到底，美国的家长会也不能算是真正意义上的家长会。学校没有强制家长们去参加，所有的活动都是大家自愿的。在老师的鼓动和美国学生对学校的热爱，每次的活动都会有很多人参加。大家都愿意牺牲自己做作业的时间，参与到学校的活动中来，每次都能带动学校的人气，正如这 Open House 一样。开放日不仅仅能向家长展示学校的面貌，更是让平日万变不离其宗的学业生活增添了几分色彩，在繁忙的学习中歇一歇，放松下来玩一玩。

异想天开的历史作业

　　我相信大家都听说过美国孩子的课题或项目（Project），最基础的便是PPT演讲。对我而言，最有挑战性、最与众不同的是我的历史课。挑战性课题的前提是要有一个想象力丰富的老师。比如——我的世界历史老师。一个学期有1～2个"大项目"，这些项目看似无厘头，其实和我们学习的内容息息相关。

　　上个学期，我们的 Project 是做一个模型。由于当时我们正在学习工业革命时期的内容，于是，我们做的这些模型都是英国工业革命时期的大发明：火车、桥、船等等。老师有一个很严苛的要求，整个模型都要亲手完成，不能用玩具火车来蒙混过关。老师会给我们将近3～4周的时间，而且全都是课外的时间来完成这个作业。首先，确定合作的成员，只要是同一个历史老师，便可以"跨班"选择好朋友一起来完成这个作业。接着，老师让我们抽签，顺序靠前的有优先选择权，最后一名只能拿剩下来的。上个学期，我虽然抽签抽到了最后一个，但选到的也是比较容易做的——运河（Canal）。紧接着的3周，便是制作模型的时间。由于大家都有各自的安排，时间很难凑到一块儿，我们便反反复复联系，敲定时间。在团队项目中，总会有很多牺牲，无论是金钱还是时间。有一个星期，我和一个同学没有空，其他的成员便去买材料，接下来的一周，我们也只抽出了一个下午大约两个小时的时间来完成这个模型。这其中，还有许多的讨论——关于怎么做最逼真。幸亏我们的审美还是比较接近，所以整个任务进行得非常顺利，最后也拿到了满分的成绩。

这个学期，老师给我们出了更大的一个难题——做一段有关于"二战"的新闻视频

150

（7～10 分钟）。站在美国的立场上，来解读"二战"时的美国到底是怎么样的，美国人都在干些什么事。这次，我们组也是同样的不幸，又抽到了最后一名。但是，我们也是幸运的，我们最想选的一个主题竟是剩下来没人要的，讲的是"二战"时的"女性劳动力"（Women in workforce）。同样给了 4 周的时间来完成。一开始可把我给愁坏了，这剪辑视频可是技术活，而且在老师给我们看的拿高分的例子中，背景都做出了演播厅的效果，难度可不是一点点。幸好，我同组不同班的好友是剪辑视频高手。

这个 Project 与上个学期又有些不同，这次分工明确，每个人都要有一个职务：1. 导演（Director），2. 查找资料的人（Researcher），3. 编剧（Writer），4. 摄影师/剪辑师（Cameraman），5. 主持人（Talent）。其实我们一开始也忙手忙脚、毫无头绪，我只查了一些资料。第一周的周五，我们组员聚在一起讨论整个新闻的形式，讨论着装。第二周的周五，我们又聚到了一起，终于开始了拍摄。我们的采访（Interview）完全是即兴的，完全没有背剧本。我当场编剧本，和大家一起讨论怎样使得整个对话更为合理。为了营造出 20 世纪 40 年代的效果，我们穿上了背带裤，扎起了头发，在车库的一角，撤掉一切"现代"的用品，营造出复古的感觉。整个采访的背景设置在一个美国的家具厂，采访工厂里正在组装门锁的工人与厂长，了解"二战"时期女性的家庭情况，工作情况……因为人手不够，我也客串了一回"厂长"，顺利地完成了外景拍摄。

如何能营造出演播厅的效果？这可让我们伤透了脑筋。最后，借助网上的新闻背景模板，投影到液晶电视上，让主持人搬个小桌子坐到电视机前，保证高度合理，还在桌子底下垫了好几本字典。正式拍摄时，为了更加的逼真，还找了配乐。记台词是一门技术活，很难一口气把一串话全都说出来，还是得靠后期剪辑效果连接起来。其中还插入了 20 世纪 40 年代的广告，和当时美国"二战"时期的女性偶像（女神）——Rosie the Reviter 的一首歌。Rosie 鼓舞所有的美国女性站出来，鼓励她们做独立富有智慧的女性。"二战"时期的女性从家庭中走了出来，走出了她们平日的生活圈（Comfort Zone），成为家庭的顶梁柱以及独立的女性。

最后放映的时候，反响不错，拿到了满分的好成绩。这个打分是由三个部分组成的：总体的视频效果占 25%，每个人的分工占 50%，组员互评占 25%。老师的打分并不是十分的严格，但是其中的艰难也是难以想象的。上传视频到 Youtube，我们的剪辑师熬夜才将视频成功上传，各种 NG……由于我们也是业余的，其中还是有些小问题，请大家多多包涵。（有兴趣观看视频的朋友可以去微信公众号"外滩教育"里找我的文章哦！）

我十分喜欢这种做 Project 的模式，一群没有拍摄视频经验的人聚在一起，一起讨论，一起摸索，最后呈现出一个好的作品。而这个 Project 给我带来更多的是快乐，繁忙课余生活的减压。希望大家能够喜欢我们的视频！

擦亮眼睛，社团水分多！

社团活动这个字眼近两年被反复提到，所有人都在讨论积极参与社团活动有助于申请好的大学。在这其中，美国的社团是所有追捧与效仿的对象，而我们学校的社团到底是什么样的呢？

每个学校情况略有不同，所以仅供参考。在每个学年开学之前，学校会发一本学生手册（Handbook），在手册里面有一年的上学日程安排、校园的活动等。如果仔细阅读的话，会发现专门有一栏是写关于社团活动的。我粗略地计算了一下，学校的社团有超过60个！大部分的社团都是课后进行活动的，但是有些选修课也是属于社团的一部分。比如说，学校的乐队、舞蹈队、戏剧都属于社团的一部分。其余的，都是一些由学生领导的课外活动。

　　由于 9 年级刚进学校没有认识很多高年级的人，经验也不足，只填写了两个社团，分别是乐队和 Paws（专门去动物避难所给小猫小狗洗澡的），结果 Paws 这个很不负责任的社团，一次活动都没有组织过，没给我发过一次邮件！所以在这里提醒大家在选社团的时候一定得和朋友多讨论讨论，才能保证社团是货真价实的！

　　美国的社团到底分几类？在我的眼里，占比最大的就是志愿者服务。其中有几个社团是全国都有的联盟社团。我们学校 PK 最厉害的是 Leo Club 和 Key Club。虽然说这两个社团的名字听上去和志愿者一点关系都没有，但他们一直在竞争，可一直没有分出个胜负来。如果你只是参加社团一个月一次的会议的话，那就一点意义都没有的。和我初中不同的是，这些社团不是学校每周挖出一个半小时的时间让同学们选一个最喜欢的社团，与志同道合的朋友一起进行活动。在美国，你想参加多少社团就能够参加多少，但分身乏术。所以我给大家的建议是，活动做得少而精。因为美国高中的学业压力很大，一直参加社团活动，没时间做作业的话，GPA 也好看不起来。在选社团的时候，要想清楚自己真正喜欢的是什么，根本没有必要参加三个几乎没有区别的志愿者服务，一直在反复做一样的事情，最后会失去兴趣。

全心全意地投入，做一个领袖，把周末留给社团。在前文也提到了，这些活动都是在课后进行的，一般都安排在周末。这也要求家长周末把时间留出来当车夫，接送孩子参与活动。很多职务都是争取来的。我的朋友 Meghan 参加了 Key Club，虽然我们都是 9 年级刚进高中的孩子，但这不代表你没有机会当社团的头儿（Officer）。我前段时间也问过她，她是怎么当上宣传部长（Publicist）的（主要负责画挂在学校的大海报）。她说刚开学的时候老师会告诉她们有选举活动（每年都会重新选举这些队长），问老师拿来申请表，然后再进行考评，通过后便顺理成章地成为了 Key Club 的宣传部长。绘画是 Meghan 的一技之长，所以想当上部长也一定要有某方面的才能。

除了志愿者俱乐部，学校还有精英俱乐部。BIBS（Brahma IB Students），Brahma Tech 就属于我们学校的精英社团（PS：Brahma 是我们学校的代表吉祥物）。IB 很好理解，进入 BIBS 这个 program 的学生在 9 年级必须要读 Biology Honors（生物荣誉班），所以参与一些社团的时候要问清楚有没有什么特殊要求。这不禁让我想起了一个朋友 Emily，我把她称为"学霸中的学霸"。她在八年级升九年级的暑假读完了 Computer System（学的是高级的 Microsoft Office 功能，因为读 Computer System 是进 Brahma Tech 的先决条件），但由于将一整个学年的内容压缩到了 6 个星期周一至周五每天 5 个半小时的课程里，教课速度极快，所以她有些作业没来得及完成，最后拿了个 B。Emily 也是 IB Students 中的一员，她在 9 年级学年里，上了 English 1 Honors（英语荣誉班），Algebra2/Trig Honors（将一个半学年的内容压缩到一个学年），Biology Honors（生物荣誉班），PE（九年级的必修课），Journalism（新闻）。在这么多门 Honor 课的压力下，她第一个学期拿了全 A，但由于暑假里上的 Computer System 拿了个 B，而且暑假里上的课的成绩，是带到下个学年的成绩单上的。所以，Emily 最后 GPA 没能拿 A，拿了3.85，但还是特别的厉害。除了学习好还不够，Emily 特别喜欢跳舞。她告诉我，每天放学后她妈妈就把她送到舞蹈房，从下午 3 点练到晚上 9 点，跳好芭蕾舞回家后再开始写作业。Algebra2/Trig 的作业又特别难，每天需要花 1～2 个小时完成，还有其他科目的作业。我没有问过她几点能够睡觉，但我相信她的睡眠时间肯定是不足的。3月底选课的时候，我问她明年的打算——两门 AP 课：Math Analysis/Calculus Honor（这门课虽然没有明说是 AP 课，但在 5 月份需要参加 AP Calculus AB 的考试）和 AP European History，其他的学科继续荣誉班。美国的孩子也是很拼的啊！

　　言归正传，给大家总结一下在报名社团活动的时候的一些要领：1. 提前在手册上预览一下学校有哪些俱乐部，而这其中又有哪些是自己个人比较感兴趣的，记下来，在开学后的社团招募活动（Club Rush）的时候不会太盲目，没有方向。2. 如果手册上没有任何信息，上学校的官网，一定会有关于社团的一栏。3. 与同学一起讨论，有共同的兴趣的就进同一个社团，这样以后也可以有个照应。4. 进了社团，积极参与，成为社团的活跃分子，和俱乐部里的小伙伴搞好关系。

5.有机会并有兴趣的话，竞选社团的领导者。做一个组织的领袖，绝对是百利而无一害的好事。

记住，在美高，千万不要做一个美国孩子最讨厌的书呆子。要多参与学校活动，多交朋友，不断地向前辈讨教经验，为自己今后做一个领袖打下地基。

老师用高科技抓住孩子们的心

如今人们离不开手机，离不开网络，离不开电脑。在学校读书也是这样，老师不再阻止我们用手机，而是鼓励我们在恰当的时候充分利用手机，因为基本上所有问题都可以用手机解决。我的生物老师就是其中的一个，她鼓励我们在课堂上多用 iPad 做练习，因为这样她收发作业方便，省了很多时间。

由于我九年级没有选生物课，读了历史（我也不知道为什么，我一直认为九年级没读生物是一个很失败的决定），所以我今年和九年级小朋友一起读生物。但是，有失必有得，我今年的生物老师非常的友善和有趣。今年也是她第一年开始教生物，她原来是化学和 AP 化学老师。

我们上课以做实验为主，每周会有 1~2

次的教课，其余时间，以小组为单位设计实验，做实验，做练习为主。老师十分鼓励各个小组之间互帮互助解决难题，实在有解决不了的问题，再去问她。

我说生物老师善于利于高科技，起因是老师提倡环保。如果我们可以把纸质练习转换为 iPad 的线上练习，这样可以节约很多纸张，我十分赞同老师的想法。可惜的是，我们生物老师辛辛苦苦节约下来的纸张，都被英语、历史和数学老师浪费完了，这些课的讲稿真的是一厚沓一厚沓发的，一点都不夸张。我的 AP 英语老师因为上课需要，经常打印一沓很厚的讲稿和试题。做完之后如果没有用，她就让我们把纸张全都扔到回收篮里，估计生物老师已经哭晕了。

首先要给大家分享我们生物课的三大法宝：Socrative，Edpuzzle，Showbie。顺便给大家介绍一下我平时经常用的几个软件。

① Socrative：每天上课之前老师总会让

我们复习一下前一天学的知识，这就是小测验的软件，输入一个教师编号，就会跳出老师准备的试题了。选好答案之后，会跳出正确答案，非常智能。唯一的缺点是你不能返回去检查做好的题目，做错了都不给修改的机会，每次点确认键的时候都胆战心惊，希望今后可以改进。

② Edpuzzle：因为我们课堂时间大部分都是用来动手做实验的，所以有许多知识点，理论课老师就会选择上传在网上让同学们自学，其中可以穿插知识点的问题。老师还自己录制教学视频，敬业，棒！基本上所有的科学老师都会使用这个平台，包括我的化学老师。因为在课上无法覆盖到的知识点，可以通过 Edpuzzle 作为一个复习、预习以及初步了解新知识的平台。因为网站构造清晰，使用流畅，令老师们爱不释手。

③ Showbie：这是我们平时课堂里最常用的一个软件了，做实验的指示，各种各样

的练习题，老师都会上传到 Showbie。我们的作业也是拍好照上传到 Showbie，老师就省去收作业这项工作了。这个软件在 iPad 上还有画画及打字的功能，等于一个文档。因为老师基本不发纸质作业，所以所有作业都要在这个软件上完成。有利有弊。虽然说携带便捷，操作方便，但更多的时候我还是觉得在纸上写下来更加踏实。

④ Google Classroom/Schoology：有的老师喜欢用 Google Classroom，有的老师爱用 Schoology，但这两个都是老师经常使用的线上交流平台。老师平常在网上布置作业并且可以把作业要求全都罗列出来，如果同学有疑问还可以在软件上提出问题让老师解答，比发邮件更方便更快捷。老师一般会把课堂上的资料全都放在软件里，所以如果有作业找不到的话，可以轻轻松松地打印出来。

连课堂小组项目都是用 iPad 完成的，用 iPad 拍视频、剪辑视频。iPad 是有无限可能性的，只有想不到，没有做不到。这就是考验老师脑洞大开的时候了。

　　生物老师唯一用纸的时候，是单元测试。而且为了做到尽可能地节约纸张，所有的考卷都是反复利用的。老师不允许我们在考卷上写字，因为所有的学生都是用同一张卷子的。老师是以身作则教育我们少用纸张，保护树木，从用 iPad 做起。（看视频还是请关注我的微信公众号，视频插入在推送中。）

美国人民真会玩

美国人民向来是会玩，每次都是出其不意，不知道他们会做什么企划，录什么视频，但是每次的视频的剪辑及配乐都能用完美形容，令人十分期待。

今天来给大家解读一下美国人的 Rally，看看美国人是有多么的会玩。Rally，发音如（R-A-Li），属于学校的特殊活动。查字典翻出来的定义是"集会"，但我总觉得和 Rally 有点出入。总的来说，Rally 将全校的学生聚集在一起，每次都有不同的主题（Homecoming、Christmas，Prom，etc.）。然后根据每次不同的主题都会有不同的舞蹈表演、乐队表演、打击乐表演。由学校的一个学生领袖组织 ASB 策划，由两名主持人将整场活动串联起来。说到底，就是整个学校的同学挤在一个并不大的体育场里开派对一样，每次的气氛都非常嗨。9、10 年级的低年级学生拘谨地坐在角落里不知所措，而 11、12 年级在另一边就兴奋起来了。明明有座位非要站着，在每次集会的高潮，每个年级都要尖叫，主持人都会用分贝仪测，看哪个年级叫得最响。当然，12 年级的同学最为激动，叫得震耳欲聋，到高兴处还会兴奋地掏出卷筒纸，在体育场的屋顶上飘呀飘。

开学的第一场 Rally 永远是 Homecoming。这是一年一度的返校舞会，所有同学都要在 Homecoming 之前选出每个年级人气最旺的男生女生作为 Homecoming Kings & Queens。这场 Rally 便成为他们展现自己才艺、为自己拉票的机会。在这 4 队中，只有一组会脱颖而出。我觉得每一场 Rally 最有趣的地方就是看 ASB 同学们准备的视频。两位主持人走进每位候选人的家里，了解他们的生活琐事（当然，这里面也包含了夸张的成分），最后剪辑好呈现在整个学校同学的面前。因为本次的 Homecoming 是以赛车场作为主题，所以两名主持人（他们都是 12 年级的学生！）还很应景地穿上了赛车服，脚上蹬着自动滑板，他们到了别人家里和像坐在自己家里一样自由自在，还不忘问人家要东西吃……

Rally 除了为大型舞会造势以外，还要为秋季运动、冬季运动、春季运动做宣传。为大家剧透一下 Spring Sports。春季运动包括棒球（Baseball）、男子游泳（Swim）、女子&男子田径（Track and Field）、女子&男子长曲棍球（Lacrosse）、男子高尔夫（Golf）、男子网球（Tennis）等。

颜值最高的非男子高尔夫球队莫属。我只有一个疑问，为什么打网球的男孩子这么黑，而打高尔夫的男孩子皮肤怎么如此白皙？我西班牙语课上有个九年级的男孩子，就是在视频里被提到的 Clay。他已经被 UCLA 录取了（commited to UCLA），因为他的高尔夫打得特别好，所以连升大学都不用愁了（人与人之间的差距）。

　　我以前不知道，长曲棍球（Lacrosse）是许多美国孩子的最爱。所以，我们学校的曲棍球队也是格外的厉害。

　　将所有的活动串在一起的是学校里的五大领袖组织（Leadership Group）之一，叫作ASB（Associated Student Body）。他们负责组织 Rally、撰写各类企划案、统一管理社团活动、在节日里装饰校园。与其他领袖组织不同的是，ASB 是一节课而其他的领袖组织都是通过午餐时间开会。因为 ASB 需要策划学校的大型活动，所以他们需要很多时间准备，拿学分也是理所应当的。

　　对于同学们来说，集会是在高压的高中生活的释放，尖叫之后，压力变小了，心情都变好了。

令人崩溃的英语课

英语课对于母语是中文的我来说，毫无疑问是最困难的，当我碰上最严厉的英语老师，难上加难。我 10 年级的英语老师，不仅仅教普通的 10 年级英语课，她还是 12 年级 AP Literature and Composition 的老师。相对于其他同年级的英语老师，她教的内容深，考的内容难。刚换到新学校，还没适应环境，就在英语课上受到了巨大的打击，难啊！

首先，说一下我们这学期读了多少东西：

① *Ray Bradbury* 小说集——一名 1920 年出生在美国洛杉矶的科幻作家，他写的作品极为科幻，内容全都和高科技、机器人、时空穿越有关。他的故事很有趣的一点是，Ray 凭着他的想象力"脑补"出来的高科技，我们现在都实现了，或是在研究开发中！每

篇故事不是很长，但是都非常好看，激动人心。我看到亚马逊上有卖，非常推荐！课上读了好几篇：*The Veldt*，*There will come soft rains*，*A sound of thunder*，*Marionettes*，*Inc*. 个人最喜欢最后一篇讲克隆技术导致夫妻之间互相欺骗的故事，结局也是出乎意料。我们老师还推荐了他写的 *Fahrenheit 451*，我还没看过，但先推荐给大家了。这本书在很多书店被推荐，高中里也是必读书目。

②*Medea*（《美狄亚》）——我们之前两个单元都没有买书，老师发邮件给我们，把 pdf 文件打印下来或者老师会在学校里打印好发给我们。*Medea* 是一部希腊神话，相比于莎士比亚的文章，*Medea* 已经被翻译成了现代英语，内容读起来也方便了很多。我个人十分喜欢这个故事，讲述了一个被丈夫背叛了的愤怒母亲，企图报复，并伤害到无辜孩子的悲惨故事。因为文章比较短，而且内容吸引人，所以读起来不会觉得很费劲。我

发现老师很喜欢给我们读关于婚姻的故事，我也不知道为什么。

③ *Macbeth*（《麦克白》）——莎士比亚写的悲剧，这大家都知道吧。讲述了 Macbeth 作为一名忠诚的国王辅佐，由于轻信了女巫算的卦，为了成为苏格兰的国王而杀害亲人的悲惨故事。这本书老师没让我们一句一句读，而是通过小组讨论以及看按照剧本演的话剧来理解整个故事。这个单元着重于写作与分析，通过人物的语言来分析一个人的品质。这本我买的是纸质书，老师建议我们读 Folger 版本的，因为注释比较多及全面。我个人十分推荐 Sparknotes 出的 NoFear 版本，因为一边是"莎士比亚时期英语"，一边是现代英语，理解起来会方便很多。

④ *The picture of Dorian Gray*（《道林·格雷的画像》）——讲述了一名爱美的英国年轻人 Dorian，想尽一切办法永葆青春，与此同时被好友 Lord Henry 灌输愤世嫉俗思想的

故事。贵族、艺术、爱情，作者使用丰富的词汇将人物形象描绘得淋漓尽致。刚开始看的时候会觉得很无聊，读不下去，但是一旦进入了语言环境，根本停不下来。这书亚马逊上有卖，推荐。但是需要有一定的英语基础，因为生词很多。

⑤ *12 Angry Men*（《12 怒汉》）——通过一件法律案件以及 12 位性格及背景截然迥异的男子坐在一起作为一支陪审团（Jury）。因为 12 位男子对一起谋杀案的看法完全不同，老师让班上 12 名同学分别来扮演这 12 名不同的男人，这样可以使同学更加投入到剧本中。通过人物带入，体验每位男子不同的视角，还原他们的立场。从判定嫌疑人有罪到嫌疑人无罪，看到了人性最深处的理智和公平公正。这还让我深入了解了美国的法律体制，了解了做陪审团是美国公民不可推卸的义务和责任。我认为这本书是每位高中生必读的。

⑥ *A Separate Peace*（《独自和解》）——以"二战"初期在美国新英格兰地区的男子寄宿高中为背景，讲述了男孩之间发生的故事。学习、体育、社交，高中男生们在成长的过程中不断地寻找自己的位置，失去了朋友又重获了朋友。那纯真时代不复存在，能够在高中生活中生存下来才是正经事。这并不是一本很长的书，所以我推荐感兴趣的可以去读一读。这也是美国文学史上的经典，我们学校 10 年级同学的必读书目。

⑦ *Lord of the Flies*（《绳王》）——飞机失事后留在一座荒岛上的一群小屁孩，自私又无知，最后在争抢食物时丢失文明，变回未开化的野人。虽然说主人公都是一群小男孩（一个女孩都没有），但是揭露的是人心深处的恐惧与自私。所有人的思想都被一个幻想中的野兽控制着，最后杀死了无辜的好友。通过阅读，我在解析阅读手法及写作对人性、无私与生存有了更加深刻的理解。

不仅仅在课堂上需要读书，我们每半个学期（Quarter）还有一本需要独自在家阅读的书（Independent Reading）。

1st Quarter：George Orwell 的 *1984*，这本名著也不需要我多做介绍了，这本书是所有十年级同学统一阅读的，在这半个学期结束后，老师出了张考卷让我们来做（说是文章最基础的内容，但其实这是骗人的，好多都是小细节!）

2nd Quarter：这个 Quarter 就可以按照自己的喜好选一本书阅读，并进行 Book talk（类似于演讲，但不是很死板的那种）。我选了 Kevin Kwan 的 *Crazy rich Asians*（《疯狂的亚洲富豪》），这是一天偶然在书店看到的，这标题太吸引人眼球了! 讲述了新加坡富豪之间明争暗斗、选媳妇的故事，太精彩了! 而且这本书词汇不是很难，非常好看，强烈推荐呢!!! 第二部 *China rich girlfriend*（《中国有钱女友》），也是我的大爱。2017 年出

了第三部 *Rich people problem*（《富豪的烦恼》），已购入。

解释一下 Book talk 是什么。老师会在你演讲前一周，发给你 5 个问题，然后你要在书中找证据，并且加上自己的理解来为全班同学介绍这本书。Book talk 的时候，老师会在 5 个问题中随机抽两个让同学来回答，所以就算老师只抽两个问题，但我还是要把每个问题的答案练习流畅。在演讲时还要克服在同学们面前演说的紧张，要和同学们有眼神交流，还要把回答控制在 1 分钟左右……

老师的 5 个问题，例如：

• Which character do you most closely resemble?（文中哪个人物与你最接近?）

• Did this book inspire you to explore new ideas or to look at things from another perspective?（这本书是否给你带来新想法或从新的视角看问题?）

• Will this book be relevant in 30 years?

（这本书在 30 年后还中肯吗?）

• Is this story driven more by character or by plot?（故事是以人物为主导还是以情节为主导?）

• What central question does the writer ask?（作者提出了什么中心问题?）

摸着良心说，作业并不算多，但是阅读与写作是家常便饭。

① 词汇。老师会发一张单子，里面会把这个单元书籍里的重点单词全都列出来，当然这不是完整的生词表，如果有不会的，还是得自己查字典。每次的单词量在20～25 个之间。看起来量比较小，但是老师会用每个词根再拓展出额外的单词，而且都得写下来，因为说不定就会出现在接下来的小测验中。我们英语老师一直和我们说，她给我们的一张张纸头都是很鲜艳的颜色，因为方便我们以后在如垃圾堆一般的书包里迅速地找到她发的资料（我觉得这个想法非常好）。虽然

有了英语注释，但是为了方便理解，我还是在旁边写上了中文。因为，每一次的单词都是来自同一本书，所以单词的语气也是相似的，很容易把单词给搞混了，而且这些英语注释都大同小异。所以，我通过中文来更好的区分。

每次小测验考整张词汇表的一半，再加上三个 Cumulative words（就是以前出现的单词，通过拼写、词性、定义来巩固），由于 cumulative 是随机的，所以每个单词都要复习到位。虽然看起来简单，但是由于不是那么明显的文字线索以及极小的题量，错两道，你就与 A 失之交臂了。

② 看书，看书，还是看书。平时没有教科书，每天都是在看书，上课讨论书里的内容，回家继续还是看书。边看书，边划重点（Annotation），这样可以帮助自己在读书的时候集中精力，不会开小差。

③ 写写写，写文章呗。不仅要会读，更

要学会写和表达。我们花了整整一个月都在写文章上面。通过小组讨论和个人写作的方式来揣摩并解析书中每个人物的内心想法。每一个章节老师都会发几段重点引用语，选择自己感觉最有共鸣的，或是最好写的，写一篇 Depth in Analysis（深度解析）。

写好后，老师收上去会选择几篇（当中有好的榜样，也有坏的）放在投影仪下让同学们指出文章中的疏漏，这样的活动能够让同学看清自身的优缺点，帮助提升写作水平。我和老师仿佛有仇一样，文章十有八九被老师放在"显微镜"（老师喜欢把投影仪叫做显微镜）下供同学阅读。当然，为了保护同学的隐私，姓名是不会暴露的。

如果你认为我们的考试就是普通的那种英语考试，那你就大错特错了。我的英语老师和年级组别的老师都不太一样，我在想这是她教 12 年级 AP 英语的缘故。她特喜欢让我们写作，而不是普通的那种死记硬背文本内容的选择题。

我们整个学年读的每一本书，几乎都是以写作来作为单元测验。因为写作是老师眼中的重中之重，所以写作占总分的比例也是最大的。

自己编短篇科幻故事、修改完善之前写的深入解析、为作文写引子，还有一个单元是演说。反正老师一直在训练我们的思维模式，通过写作、演说来理清我们的思路。

但是期末考试由于要全年级统一，老师终于出了一张选择题的卷子给我们做。考前，老师给了我们复习范围，但这给了等于没给。意思就是说：请你将我这学期发的五颜六色的纸都看一遍。我就只能把基础给复习到位，大量复习词汇以及考前的练习。老师也提醒了我们，词汇是期末考的重点。老师没骗我们，期末考试的着重点的确放在了词汇上，占到 65% 以上。

关于英语课这件事，完全是看运气，看

你碰到什么老师。有的同学是轻轻松松拿 A，而在我老师的课上拿 A 非常难。但对我来说，这也是不断尝试与提高的一年，更多的是感恩。

毕业后他们的去向

12 年级的同学毕业了。毕业典礼那天，Instagram 上偶然刷到几张照片。看！人家"网红们"在学士服里穿了这么好看的裙子！

每年学校都会出一本杂志，深扒同学内幕，统计他们进了什么大学、他们高中 4 年干了点什么、学校里有多少对情侣，最后将所有内容汇总，写出一本 senior issue（12 年级大事件）。这是一年的重头戏，因为这里面囊括了所有毕业生的去向，全校 GPA 前 2%优秀毕业生的告别演说（valedictorians），以及所有即将毕业的运动队队员的照片。每年都有一张美国地图，地图的两侧标注了每位学生决定前往的大学。

经过统计，今年有很多学生进入了加州的好大学。加州大学洛杉矶分校 UCLA（11

人），加州大学伯克利分校 UCB（21 人），南
加州大学 USC（21 人）。当然，热门的学校
也不仅仅在加州：科罗拉多大学 University
of Colorado，Boulder（22 人）；华盛顿大学
University of Washington（12 人）；亚利桑那
大学 University of Arizona（17 人）。学校也
不乏进入常春藤顶尖学校的人，我将 2015 年
与 2016 年的常春藤录取人数做成表格更直接
地展现给大家看：

大学名称（College name）	2015	2016
布朗（Brown）	2	2
哥伦比亚（Columbia）	0	0
康奈尔（Cornell）	1	1
达特茅斯（Dartmouth）	1	0
哈佛（Harvard）	2	2
宾大（U Penn）	0	2
普林斯顿（Princeton）	3	2
耶鲁（Yale）	2	1
麻省理工（MIT）	0	2

大学名称（College name）	2015	2016
斯坦福（Stanford）	1	1
范德堡（Venderbilt）	1	3
约翰霍普金斯（John Hopkins）	1	1
杜克（Duke）	1	1
总计人数（Total）	15	18

　　表格里没有囊括所有进名校的人，也有同学进了卡内基梅隆大学、西北大学等，这里仅仅是选了几所标志性的前20名大学，分享一下数据。

　　我个人也在研究这些进常春藤的同学们，他们的敲门砖是什么？凭什么名牌大学选择了他们而不是其他人？在一年一本的Yearbook（校历）里，我找到了答案：体育好！基本上都是因为体育好被名牌大学录取了。姐妹花双双进入MIT，她们是学校的划船队成员（Crew）；帅哥们大学在普林斯顿和哈佛继续打排球（Volleyball）；前往哈佛大学踢足球

(Soccer)；去布朗大学打曲棍球（Lacrosse）；到 Claremont McKenna 跑步（Track & Cross Country）；在 UCLA 打水球（Waterpolo）等等。虽然说进了名牌大学，但是这些同学还要保证在大学 4 年为校队效力，因为他们从一开始就是通过体育优秀而被大学录取的。又是被"套牢"4 年。

没有人天生就会打篮球、踢足球，所以他们的成功离不开从小开始的培养和训练，以及高中不懈的努力，只有这样才能获得进入名校为校队效力的机会。虽然他们属于体育生，但这不代表他们的学习不好，只是相对来说，大学招生官对他们成绩的要求会比其他申请者宽松。

除了凭借体育实力进入名牌大学的同学，学校里还有 TOP 2%，整个年级里被选出来的最优秀的 8 个同学，作为告别演说者（Valedictorians）。2016 年的这 8 位，4 人进了加州大学伯克利分校（UCB），一位进了斯坦福大学（Stanford），一位进了南加州大学（USC），一位进了波莫纳学院（Pomona），还有一位进了宾夕法尼亚大学沃顿商学院（Wharton School @ University of Pennsylvania）。这8位学生表达了他们对学校的感激之情，部分学生将他们在大学的专业写在了演说词里，有读数学、生物的，也有读商科的。

这8位同学有着共同的特点，他们在高中期间都参加了丰富的学校活动，是学校领袖组织（Leadership Group）的一员，积极参与社团及社区活动，成绩好。比我高一届的（2017届）学校 ASB 主席，是需要选举才能当选的。虽然说他的社会活动很多，但是他的成绩并不是最好，所以他只进了 Texas Christian University（德克萨斯基督教大学），没有我预想中的好。我认为如果能够做这种大型领袖社团的主席，他可以被录取到更好的大学，但是他选择了 Early Decision（提前申请），进了 Texas Christian University，说明成绩不够理想。所以在进行社团活动的同时，也要保持良好的成绩。

　　看着一届一届同学毕业，总觉得离我毕业也越来越近。毕业后的我将去向何方？

11 年级的开学感想

新学年的开学总是忙忙碌碌，最主要还是从假期模式慢慢调回 6:30 起床的上课模式，忙着进行社交生活，适应新老师和新课程。

开学首先是忙学习。今年没给自己太多压力（例如读 4 门 AP 的朋友们大有人在），两门 AP（计算机科学和英语），两门荣誉课程（化学与数学）。我们学校的荣誉课程（Honors）也有 GPA 加分，满分为 4.5（普通课程为 4.0，AP 为 5.0）。

最具挑战性的还是 AP。首先是计算机科学（Computer Science），完全没有接触过的 java 编程。在全民学 STEM 的影响与熏陶下，我大胆地选了这门课。开学这一个多月以来受益匪浅。虽然我们学校的编程老师不怎么好（他半年前才开始自学 java），幸亏课堂上还有经验丰富的程序员助教，配合网上的练习以及同学们的互帮互助。我有一次在课堂上捕捉到两位男同学单膝下跪与另一名男同学交流课堂作业的情形。

我认为做程序猿最大的魅力是写程序与思考的过程，要有钻研的精神，不放弃，才能做出最后想要达到的结果。我经常一边盯着电脑，一边盯着书，研究如何写出简洁有效的程序或是找出程序运行错误的原因。最开心的时候就是当我独自写出了正确的程序。但是，程序出错的可能性对于我这种初学者更为常见。老师说，当程序越写越长，写的时候更要小心，因为修改起来很复杂，有时需要重头开始写，重写。

如果希望培养强大的逻辑思维能力，AP Computer Science 是你最好的选择。今年我们班上只有 7 个女孩子，所以我要鼓励所有的女孩子，若有兴趣的话，可以尝试编程！

（但是，我大学不会往这个方向发展，我只是希望可以懂这方面的知识。）

AP（Language and Composition），英语课，以阅读理解、写作、修辞手法的解析为重点，对于我从小在中国长大的孩子来说，并不是最容易的一门课。但是特别幸运的是，我今年有一位十分美丽又善解人意的英语老师。她在暑假里就与另一位 AP 英语老师拟定好了一整年的学习计划，所以目前所有的学习都在有条不紊地进行中。暑假加上开学，已经读了三本书，包括剧本、语法及非虚构小说。我个人最喜欢那本非虚幻小说 *Into the Wild*（《荒野生存》），有兴趣的可以看这本书，或者同名电影。主要内容是说一个年轻人为了寻找真相，前往阿拉斯加冒险的故事。

每周最让人头疼的是 Multiple Choice Monday（选择题周一），老师会随机抽一篇 AP 的阅读理解，按照题目的数量给出相应的时间（有 10 道选择题，就给 10 分钟阅读并答题）。很多时候题目看得云里雾里，只能靠运气——蒙答案。同样令人头疼的还有看文章及限时 40 分钟的写作。这个话题就不展开了，有兴趣可以阅读前文，我有详细介绍英语课。这门课需要大量阅读，若阅读是弱项，建议绕道。

课余：学校各项活动还是照常进行，该怎么玩就怎么玩。

化学课和数学课是荣誉班，但是目前来说没什么大问题。西班牙语也不是特别难，毕竟我才读 2 级。

再说说美国历史。我读的是普通的美国历史，我没有选择 AP US History 的原因是学校的这位 AP 历史老师是同学们口中十分严厉的一个人，如果老师和你没有对上眼，你的一整年都会十分痛苦。因为难度很大，我身边去年读 AP 世界历史的朋友今年选的都是普通历史。我也选择了普通美国历史。内容还是比较容易理解的，只是考试考得比较频繁（两周一章节）。

　　我们的历史和英语老师一直在鼓励我们看总统辩论以及大选的现状。因为4年一次的大选是美国的大事，而且这两位候选人势均力敌，不到最后，不好说谁赢。我在阅读《时代周刊》的文章时，看到有数据表明，希拉里已经完全在 Millennials（千禧年，普遍指18—34岁）中站稳脚跟，获取了大部分年轻人的选票（也是摇摆票中的重头）。可惜最后还是输给了川普，与总统失之交臂。

　　平衡日常生活和学习是我在11年级学习的一堂课，因为课上老师会布置有难度的作业，虽然量不多，但是需要时间思考，需要学习 SAT，还需要参加丰富的社团活动。我还在寻找三者之间的平衡点，不断地调整状态。

　　高中的课内与课外平衡点不是那么容易掌握的，但这是高中生活必不可少的经历。缺少了挑战的高中生活是不完整的。

后　记
Afterword

　　我的第一个平台是"外滩教育"（大家有兴趣的可以关注公众微信号"外滩教育"）给我的。9年级的某一天，妈妈问我要不要给"外滩教育"写文章，我说好啊，然后就成了专栏"小留学生日记"的一员。不限题材，每月定期交稿，还有稿费拿，在初中并不是才女的我居然成了自由撰稿人！吴慧雯老师也一直鼓励我，说我的文章质量在逐步提高，有时阅读量还不赖。现在回看之前写的文章，我也经常反问自己，怎么文笔这么幼稚？但我也不难发现我的写作内容越来越丰富了，正文思路也变得渐渐清晰。有了老师的鼓励，于是我在10年级开学时创立了自己的公众号。虽然粉丝量并不多，但我很看重这个平台，因为从标题、排版、照片都是我自己选，选我喜欢的音乐是写推文过程中最快乐的事。

我从小并没有表现出对写作的巨大热爱，但我特别爱看时尚杂志，看《伊周》是我每周最期待的一件事。从小学开始每周买杂志，阅读每季新潮流、封面人物、八卦新闻，时尚杂志及我最爱的电影《穿普拉达的女魔头》让我对成为时尚杂志编辑产生了无限憧憬。很不幸，2016年底《伊周》停刊了。纸媒的日趋衰弱让我对新媒体与科技产生了浓厚的兴趣，这也是我一直运营公众号的一大原因。新媒体是未来的发展方向，如何让高科技和新媒体更好地结合是我未来想要研究的方向（因为我爱上了编程）。

我书中的故事写的都是一些校园里的小事，那些真实发生的新鲜事。公众微信号就是我的平台，让我把我看到的通过写作的方式传达给那些没有机会体验美国高中生活的人。看完文章之后，有人会想：啊，美国高中生活居然是这样的！从校园小事说起，让读者变成我，然后感受美国高中的氛围。

每个人的美高生活都很相似却又有所不同，所以你也会疑惑你们学校的舞会与我们学校的舞会不一样，但这并没有关系。如果我们的高中生活都是一模一样那就没有意思了，高中就是要体验新鲜的、不同寻常的生活。刚入学最棘手的还是社交，如何找到志同道合的朋友？如何与外国孩子交朋友？如何融入美高生活而不是整天和说中文的孩子抱成一团？这几个问题是没有答案的，我也给不出一个标准答案。但你一定要去尝试与同学聊天，不能胆怯，即使英语不够流利也不要自卑。换个角度思考，你这些美国同学有几个会说中文？有机会锻炼英语是一种馈赠，提高英语说到底还是得靠自身在学习及交友上的努力。

《美高新鲜事》正如 Megan 所说，不能解决"美国天气怎么样"这个问题，但是这本书可以带你走入美高幕后的那些故事。在阅读完整本书后，还请你们自己总结中美教育的相似及不同之处。作为一个经历过中国和美国教育的学生，我欣赏并感激中美教育。你的结论是什么？

谢谢我的伯乐——豪叔，如果没有遇见您，今天我将会是在哪里？若是当初没有您支持我读美高，说不定我现在还在上海做一名备战高考的高中生呢！

还要谢谢一路上支持我的爸爸妈妈和家人，关注我的那些朋友，还有我自己。

My first writing platform was given by Bund's Education. Mom asked me if I would like to write for Bund's Education about my high school life in America，I accepted and became one of their many student writers. I could write on any topic as long as I submitted one article every month and I received remuneration for writing! The girl who was not the most poetic in middle school became a freelancer! I would like to thank editor Wu who encourages me and tells me that my writing improves over time and she notices that more people read my articles. When I look back at my articles written in Freshman year, I constantly ask myself, "What am I writing about? Why were my thoughts all over the place?" As time proceeds, I found my writing becomes more coherent and logical which is a good sign. I find my personal style of writing and add my own twist to a coverage. With my parents and editor's encouragement, I made a big decision in the fall of 2015—I created my personal official account on Wechat (Wechat is equivalent to Facebook in China with more than 800 millions active users). There are not many followers but I love this platform because I get to decide the heading, layout, pictures, and the best part is to choose the background music for the post.

Although I was not the most passionate writer

when I was young, I was obsessed with Fashion magazines. Reading *Femina* is the most exciting activity of the whole week since elementary school. I would run to the newspaper stand after class, buy the magazine, and read it while I walked home. From reading new trends of the season, cover stars' stories, and the gossip news along with my all‑time favorite movie——*The Devil Wears Prada*——inspired me to become a fashion editor. Unfortunately, *Femina* discontinued at the end of 2016. The end of press era signaled the uprising new media and technology and it is one of the reason why I run my personal official account now. New media is the future, and I would love to learn the perfect way to combine technology and New media into a new form of communication in the future since I love media and coding.

The stories in this book are all small episodes of my daily life at school, the novelties happened at school. The official account gives me the platform to speak to those who don't have the opportunity to experience the American high school life in my writing. After reading my articles, some may exclaim, "Ah, this is the real life of an American high schooler!" These lightbulb moments are the most precious! From my writing, readers get to substitute into my position and experience my typical life at school.

Everybody's high school life is similar yet different therefore it is okay if you school's Prom differed from mine. If all of our high school lives are the same, it would be boring and mundane. High school is all about experience new and unusual things. I struggled to find friends when I first transferred to Corona del Mar High School. How to find friends that are like-minded? How to make friends with Americans? How to blend into the American culture instead of sticking with friends who speak Mandarin? There are no answers to these questions, I could not provide standard answers either. The best advice I would say is to try, try to talk to your classmates even though you are scared. Don't be discouraged if you cannot speak fluent English. From a different perspective, do your friends speak better Mandarin than you do? You are blessed to be bilingual. You are gifted with the opportunity to practice English in American High School but you have to work hard and go out of your comfort zone to improve your English to a whole new level.

Like what Megan said in the beginning of the book, *Behind the Scenes* may not give you the answer to "How is the weather like in the U.S." but this book takes you to the "backstage" of the daily lives of American High School. I hope you can learn one thing or two after reading this book and draw a conclusion about the similarities and differences of Chinese and American High Schools. I am blessed with the opportunity to experience both types of educations and I appreciate both of them. What is your conclusion?

I cannot forget to thank Uncle Howard, my

talent scout. Without your encouragement，I still might be an ordinary high school student in Shanghai instead of studying abroad in the United States!

I have to thank my parents and family members for supporting me the entire time and my friends for reading my articles from the bottom of my heart.

At last，I would also like to thank myself.

陈贝婷

Beiting (Betty) Chen

图书在版编目(CIP)数据

美高新鲜事 / 陈贝婷著. —上海：文汇出版社，
2017.8

ISBN 978 - 7 - 5496 - 2277 - 1

Ⅰ.①美… Ⅱ.①陈… Ⅲ.①高中-留学生教育-概
况-美国 Ⅳ.①G639.712.8

中国版本图书馆 CIP 数据核字(2017)第 188695 号

美高新鲜事
Behind The Scenes

陈贝婷
Beiting (Betty) Chen / 著

责任编辑 / 竺振榕
封面装帧 / 赵　军

出版发行 / 文汇出版社
　　　　　上海市威海路 755 号
　　　　　（邮政编码 200041）
经　　销 / 全国新华书店
排　　版 / 南京展望文化发展有限公司
印刷装订 / 苏州市越洋印刷有限公司
版　　次 / 2017 年 8 月第 1 版
印　　次 / 2017 年 8 月第 1 次印刷
开　　本 / 787×1092　1/32
字　　数 / 80 千字
印　　张 / 6.875(彩色插页 8)

ISBN 978 - 7 - 5496 - 2277 - 1
定　　价 / 35.00 元